Beyond the Dream Horse

A Revealing Perspective on Attaining a True Relationship

By

Michael Bevilacqua

First paperback edition published 2010.

ISBN 10: 1453725261
ISBN 13: 9781453725269

Cover photo by Michael Bevilacqua

Table of Contents

*

*

Thanks to JR Big Leo for choosing me and with his big heart, humour and patience, opened my eyes and soul

Table of Contents

*

*

*Thanks to JR Big Leo for choosing me and with his big heart,
humour and patience, opened my eyes and soul*

Foreword

Some horse books are educational, some are inspirational and some, like this one, are both. Bevilacqua, who is Canadian, describes his decade-long journey of discovery as a horseman that started when he was middle-aged. A record of a mature individual's first encounter with horses is unusual. If that person has not been blind-sided by tradition, has an enquiring mind and a gift for observation, it is likely to be refreshing. Bevilacqua has all these qualities. His story has a special interest because the decade in which his journey occurred, 2000 to 2010, happens to be a landmark in the 5000 year history of horsemanship. As he writes, it was a period during which a 'wave of change' occurred.

Starting out as a new but questioning horse owner at 37, the author relates his early experience with traditional horse management and moves on to test Pat Parelli's programs, Monty Roberts' Join-Up, and other methods. He adopts none of these but he does adopt barefoot management. Early on he discards the bit in favour of a halter, discards the halter in favour of the crossunder bitless bridle, and – in the passage of time – discards the crossunder bitless bridle in favour of a cordeo. From being a novice horse owner, he becomes a trainer 'by request', a BitlessBridle representative, and helps to launch the international forum of the Nevzorov Haute Ecole website. Initially a pleasure rider, he becomes a trail rider, develops an interest in dressage and ultimately prefers to interact with horses on the ground to develop the partnership he seeks.

As a trainer, he claims no formal 'method'. He avoids training routines aimed at producing obedient-humble-servants in favour of a positive reinforcement approach that fosters trust and willing cooperation. His relationship with a horse is not that of teacher and pupil. His approach might be characterized by three pillars of wisdom: listen with love to the horse, have faith in your interpretation of the horse's feelings, and communicate rather than control. In two words, make friends.

Readers are given insights into how Alexander Nevzorov achieves his dream relationship with a horse. Beyond this, they learn about Bevilacqua's personal discoveries regarding the nature of the horse. They learn, for example, that friendship with a horse is not transferable to another person. Along the way, readers may discover a new world and that riding becomes "just a tiny part of what is possible."

- Robert Cook, FRCVS, PhD, Professor of Surgery Emeritus, Tufts Cummings School of Veterinary Medicine; Chairman BitlessBridle Inc.; Co-author *Metal in the Mouth – The Abusive Effects of Bitted Bridles.*

Introduction

Contrary to the many shades of grey in modern life, feelings are quite simple. They are good, or not. Aside from regret, a sense of loneliness, or frustration, anger, solitude, sadness can emerge when our brains and our hearts follow diverging paths. I hope that these writings will help to give even greater value to your own feelings about sensing what is right for you and your horse. It may prove invaluable for anyone thinking about getting their first horse. The ability to bring about desired changes is not all so complicated or obscure as it may seem. It is my hope that this book will give you the strength and courage and confidence to follow your own instinct. It is not easy to cast off all that has accumulated within us during a lifetime. There is a lot of clutter that suppresses and diminishes the flame within our hearts for many things. Most often, a flame continues to flicker, buried somewhere deep within us.

The expectations between people and horses are quite ingrained in our own psyche. We tend to adhere to the past and what we know or what is learned, or standards with which we grew up or are accustomed. It is often much more simple to do so than to deal with a new realization that is before our very eyes, or in our hearts. Yes, even when we are seeking it. It is denial or selfishness, or maybe even fear. It is not easy to wander off the beaten path when everyone is calling out and pointing the usual way back. We so often ignore our own feelings and do not appreciate the wellspring of our own experiences as a reality that can truly exist. In turn, sometimes even our own realizations, without support, can simply fade away behind the noise of daily life. We can feel lost. At one point, I did.

It is my goal to present a different perspective so that others can begin to live with new insight, not only about themselves, but also about their horses. The possibility that has so often been overlooked has always existed. The focus here is not on any particular training technique, types of equipment, or even scientific research. Although such points are touched upon through the course of my own learning experience, this is primarily about the relationship. This is a rediscovery rather than presenting anything new or groundbreaking regarding horses. Everyone holds the potential to see with new eyes and renewed spirit.

I cannot help but recall the horses that passed through my life. Those horses were to help people to fulfill their dreams. People asked me, an outsider, to make those particular dreams come true. How so different the reality was with those horses that were not my own. How beautiful was our shared brief time together. It inevitably changed my life.

Most of the horses came from some other life. It was a life where they were considered inadequate, unpredictable. After harsh, attempted indoctrination into the accepted human norm of what a horse should be, and failure to adjust, many horses were eliminated or cast off. Once labelled as `crazy`, then crazy they could become through neglect or isolation. They were considered as unbroken, or unbreakable, or using the newer term, could not be gentled. However, selling them to new owners was more profitable than putting them up for auction to go to the slaughterhouse. Those who survived that phase ended up in the lives of the new, hopeful owners. In consequence, they often were viewed in a new life as inadequate and unpredictable, and, therefore, dangerous. Usually the buyers were first-time horse owners, and they both ended up in my life.

A few horses that I have known over the course of my giving training or classes are highlighted here because of the impact they had on my view of horses in general. I was granted a little piece of paradise by those surviving, magnificent horses. Horses of feeling and kindness, humour, peace, curiosity, patience, character, understanding and willingness to try - regardless of their past.

For the people, the pursuit of the dream horse was becoming a reality. Unfortunately, although the horses had a new chance, whenever the clock was ticking for that dream to coalesce, in the end, one way or another, the horses paid the price.

The experience of my time with some of these fantastic horses is my story. It is their story. All we can do is to share with the world around us. Yet, at the same time, it tells of the possibility of a beauty that can be found and has been found by some.

This will not merely be an account of my experiences with horses, but, rather, what I have learned from those experiences. The results are much more important for me than to simply recount a story. I do not mean results, or performances, that were attained by the horses. There will be many important differentiations about the meanings of words as they pertain here. This is very important to understand. There are some meanings of words that go off onto a slightly different tangent than what is standard lingo in the horse world. The challenge is to explain what I mean when I try to describe something learned from horses. Yet, I believe those who have had similar experiences will easily understand it. Secrets and treasures of the heart are not easily described. Pure emotion of the spirit is not readily understood. Yet, there are people scattered throughout the world who will understand *exactly* what I describe. It is almost a phenomenon that those numbers have been steadily growing in recent years.

The following stories contain both good and bad but that is only relating to the general surface of the circumstances. From my perspective, there was always something that I learned that was either heartbreaking or stunningly beautiful. It is often too easy to generalize in trying to make a point, but it is often unfair. However, in some instances outside of my personal experiences, I do see a similar attitude or reaction appear over and again.

No owners ever consider themselves cruel. Yet, the horses, to some, were as useful and disposable, as non-refillable lighters. The horses could also simply be a very big disappointment based on people's personal, emotional expectations. The sad side of what I witnessed came from those who wanted to pursue their dream, but were unable to dedicate time or personal effort to the horse they claimed to love. What they really seemed to love was the feeling that they pursued. A lifelong dream or emptiness within themselves or their lives, somewhere, they seemed to need to fill. I am not writing about people who may purchase a horse to fit into some social crowd or as a commodity. The lack of interest in the horse is obvious. The stories here include those who all have different backgrounds, lifestyles and varied ages, and were all seeking something indescribable, yet, at the same time, very real. Although the people played a role, this is mainly about the horses.

Sometimes, reality before our own eyes is not good enough to erase the label given to a horse by others who personally know nothing about that particular horse. Words in whispered barn talk could eventually erase wondrous, personal experience of elation and happiness from cherished moments with the horse. In some cases, to the detriment of hopeful horse owners, what people talked about was considered truth. Then the slightest slip in acceptable behaviour from the horse could become the focal point of a total and complete turn away from the dream. The same applies to not following the norm. The more focused people are on what they do not want or their fears, the worse it gets, and the more isolated the horse becomes. I have witnessed situations deteriorate due to fear where the owner would stop trying to personally learn and hand the horse over to a severe trainer for `correction`. From there, it only became a search or anticipation for unwanted behaviour. Some of these horses endured that, and it was pointless to repeat the same approach because that is why they were cast off and bought cheap to begin with. The horse was doomed, no matter the good days of joy and pleasure and soaring heights of spirit previously enjoyed by the owner or the progress of the horse. The pursuit of the dream horse sometimes became a twisted romanticism. Fear won. Self-doubt won. Those seeking it as a type of package to be handed to them seldom attained the dream.

Impatience in humans, and lack of communication, expression, clarity, and knowledge, even social expectations and pressure, can be lethal - for horses.

The good side is that a large majority of people are beginning to think twice. Science has provided factual results that give justification to changes in the management of horses. Health facts that are pertinent today now that we do not have to rely on live horsepower to survive. Training facts that many people already started to have a doubting feeling about, but had no real reason to change. There are facts to which some people are still completely oblivious or refuse to accept. Although much has changed, it is unlikely that humankind will be unanimous in their views about horses or anything else. Nevertheless, there are some universal feelings and we are all human.

I present facts or situations that many in the horse world would say is impossible for horses to achieve. It is my hope that the examples and the research given will open up the possibility of, at least, changing some of our fixed ideas or beliefs. Many research facts have existed for a long time without having much impact on changing our own behaviour toward horses. The most significant and rewarding changes arise from the people themselves. Some of the greatest achievements between people and horses have nothing to do with science or research.

With the growing awareness that I have lived and witnessed worldwide in such a short time, instinct, to me, now means following that little voice or feeling within our hearts, or taking time to ponder the look from a horse's eye. Maybe, in the same sense, it really means being very honest with ourselves. Ironically, taking time to observe and reflect instead of seeking answers outside of ourselves may bring us much closer to ourselves, horses, nature and what we want, than we ever imagined possible. In the world that we live, it can be one of the most difficult journeys to pursue. That fragile, subdued flame within our hearts struggles against the oppressive, surrounding norms. This is your chance to bring it back to life.

Following an instinct, in this case, does not mean to be an animal. However, it is by reaching our true inner selves that we do come closer to that. Lest we forget, that is what we are. Maybe not. It is just a word. It is man who gives classification. What I refer to is our true selves, not how we have been conditioned to live in our world. It is man, in his belief of superiority over everything in this world, who has created most of the problems that we aspire to overcome. There are many catch-22`s in life. We are one of them. It does not have to be that way.

At First Glance

Although I had looked into most of the different training methods out there, I did not adhere to any specific one. In working with a young horse with no saddle experience, I had no prescribed methodology nor adhered to techniques to force my way through any panic or defiance issues with the horse. I would do the same if it were an older horse with people issues. I would back off before it ever got to such a state. The trainers that people find most impressive are the ones who can make a horse comply in the shortest time possible. I never strived to achieve one particular task within one session. I suppose I allowed the horse to tell me what was acceptable at any given time. In the views of most people, that does not make a very good trainer. The horses, however, literally begged to differ.

When I finally owned my own horse, I will always recall a momentary eye contact that occurred at the end of a training session under saddle. He was still at the place where I bought him and was still going through basic training with one of the people who worked there. The owner of the place remains to this day, one of my greatest inspirations of my life with horses. Although mostly traditional, she offered a lot of insight, encouragement and tips from her experience and knowledge about horses outside the realm of a training pen.

At the end of a training session where we were practicing trotting under the scrutinous eye of the trainer, three other horses that were with us, left the arena. The trainer had us doing another lap as the door to the arena was open and the other horses were filing out with the owners. My horse definitely wanted to follow the others and headed for the door. I could feel how desperate he was for this. He did not charge out with me on board, but it was very clear that he would not stay alone in the arena. He was born and raised in open space in Shamrock, Saskatchewan, Canada, with dozens of other horses. We had a good session and I was fine with that. It was not fine with the trainer. She closed the door and tried to regain my horse's attention. She did not want a herd-bound horse and I was supposed to be the boss. She insisted that I mount again and finish that one lap. The horse was in a panic. He was neither angry nor aggressive, but he seemed terrified. I watched as the trainer struggled from the ground with reins in hand and I could plainly see that the only mounting that was going to happen was her anger. I think what made it worse was that she may have felt slightly embarrassed because this horse challenged her professionalism, or rather, diminished it to onlookers. She began to shout and yank the reins attached to the Pelham bit. My horse reared up and as he did so, with his eyes wide with fear and pain, he looked at me. It shocked me. It was how he looked at me. It was only for a moment, but I saw a plea for help. A hope that maybe I, really practically a stranger, could do something. Even though I found the entire panic situation unpleasant, even understood that he did not want to be without other horses, it was based only on the physical reactions that I was seeing. I did not really attribute feelings to my horse. That is why that momentary glance surprised me so. I really felt his message. It hit me like a ton of bricks. It was the first time a horse `talked` to me so clearly. Maybe, it was the first time I noticed.

This example is only one of the little moments that began to forge my own reality with horses. I never voiced my dislike of what I saw in training stables, I just decided to do things differently. However, that was not the day that everything really changed.

It is not that I had a plan or considered myself a better trainer. I did not consider myself a horse trainer at all. For the first time, I started to realize that what was really going on in the world around me was a great contrast to my initial idea of what having a horse meant. The reality that my horse was living was not the beauty and dream of what drew me to horses. I saw this in every subsequent stable in which he was boarded. Look at any large stable, take a snapshot of the alley. It is very similar to a prison cellblock. Yet, how are horses usually depicted? They are free and running. Even stables could have beautiful names and logos of winged horses or comical smiling horses or a horse running free in a field. Not so in the real world, is it? It goes even beyond that with how we deal with horses every day. Yet, I was also trapped in the norm. Despite our feelings that may creep in from time to time, we are constantly reminded through social pressure. No one, at any of the stables that we were at, thought as I did.

The fraction of a second where my horse reached out to me that day rearing in the arena, stayed with me. I was not the same. It was not an instantaneous deliberate, conscious decision, but it certainly was a guiding factor in all subsequent decisions. Social confrontations of standard, repeated stable talk of leader, boss, and stopping the horse at every perceived, thought out, deliberate move increasingly became annoying to me. With what existed around me in the horse world, I felt that I did not know enough. Yet, most of my actions were based on a tiny spark within my heart, from not only that day in the arena, but also, how I came to choose my horse in the first place. Although it may sound cliché, I can say he chose me.

I had gone to the ranch to look at a Canadian horse. I had decided on a black, strong build. I could see strong bone features and muscle shimmering in the light, standing atop a hill with thick mane blowing in the wind. In any case, when I walked alone into the stable to the designated box of the Canadian, I saw and felt, even then, something not right with that horse. What I felt, and I do recall this very well, is that the horse seemed to want to get close, yet and the same time, was overwhelmed and distrustful or afraid. It may have had something to do with the horse behind me, but that is only in retrospect. Again, it was just something in the eye and face and overall body signals, yet, very subtle behaviour. At the time, it was just an impression. It was similar to meeting someone with shifty eyes. I backed off and paced the alley and right across from the Canadian was JR Big Leo. Never did I think of a multi-coloured horse. He approached the steel bars with a look I can still not quite describe. His whole demeanour won my heart. I still tried to approach the Canadian, and went back and forth between my `dream` horse and Big Leo for almost an hour. I came in search of my perfect image of a

Canadian and not only did I leave that image of a dream behind, I left that stable with the Paint horse, JR Big Leo, as my new-found companion.

Although I had experiences before with other horses, just in passing, he was the beginning of my journey into truth. So many other attitudes and phrases exist today, regarding horses. Most often, they only continue to serve human ego and one-sided emotional fulfillment. In my case, it was the opposite. It was the falling away of pre-conceived notions and standard behaviour. This was an ongoing process. A subtle process was taking place within.

Now let us fast forward in time. Once Leo was out of horse boot camp, he easily realized the difference between a standard trainer and me. I had discovered that, although he would accept the bit, he would not let me mount while he was wearing a bitted bridle. I was never nervous and constricted on horseback and when I rode him at the place where I bought him, I always kept a loose rein. However, through his actions, he was talking to me now. He was presenting a scary charade where I had to narrow down what he was trying to specify.

Those who would witness his behaviour gave me the usual suggestions. Most often, the advice was that I needed a more severe bit. Looking at different models, I could not believe some designs, made of metal, to be placed among soft tissue. The twisted and spiked bits stayed in the store. I barely got on him once we were on our own and I started to feel fear when I did. I still remembered the one time he went rodeo on me in boot camp clear across the arena. When he turned at the wall, he went one way and I went the other. I was crumpled in the sand with three bruised ribs. I also remember that it was the first time that someone else saddled him that day, and it was the last time that I would allow anyone else to do anything that I should be doing.

Regarding the bit, like most of my learning, it happened by accident, and it was Leo who showed me. I noticed that he would be very relaxed when only in a halter, and if I tried to mount, it did not seem to be a problem. That solved it for me on the spot. I would remove the bit. People thought I was crazy.

I went further. By the time we left the ranch, he could be ridden at walk and trot. We had never cantered or galloped. We had some finishing work to do. In a halter with the reins clipped on, the square, metal piece along the cheek would rotate into his face when I did an open rein. That started to bother me, so I went in search of something else. I found Dr. Cook's cross-under Bitless Bridle.[1] For what it achieved for me and with Leo's obvious approval of it, I became a representative. Nothing changed regarding people's opinions about me riding without a bitted bridle. They thought it was pure folly and I even endured lectures from stable mates who, with good intentions, would try to dissuade me from going bitless. It was not their opinion that counted for me. It was Leo's acceptance. That opened a completely new path for me. People just watching me and Leo, and eventually, our other horses, started to ask me to train theirs. I ended up becoming a horse trainer by circumstance. Nevertheless, there was still a lot of learning that would take place along the way.

Communicating like a Horse

Ready, set, pin your ears. A person believing to be talking a horse language is quite popular. It is all based, supposedly, on herd behaviour and horse psychology. In other words, using wild horse behaviour, how horses interact with each other, and then applying the same technique when trying to communicate, or usually, subdue horses - to get the horses to do what humans want.

Humans, in their own desire to believe that they can outwit and dominate any other creature on earth, including the most perceptive of all animals on the face of the planet, will ignore the latter fact, and pretend to be a horse to another horse.

We tend to believe what we think and can base any information to any desired, self-convinced end. If we really look hard enough, we do always see what we are looking for.

How many times have you heard: `Humans are predators, horses are prey`? We have the eyes straight forward for hunting and horses have eyes on the side for lookout... etc. Not wrong, but, have you ever seen a lioness grooming herself among grazing horses? It happens.

How we so complicate our lives with all the analysis that goes into a human conjecture. How people capitalize on such studies, perhaps eventually see only one erroneous aspect, seek them or create them, and then later on, we find that not all is quite right. A new horse study comes out providing physiological data that proves quite contrary to our interpreted observation. It happens with humans, too. At least studies tend to advance and become more scientific and subjective. Each advance continues to pick apart our own initial beliefs.

Humans have the capability of love and, at the same time, unspeakable atrocities. We do all have a streak of barbarism in us regardless of our advancements. Yet, we seem to keep looking for intellectual studies, while our world is in shambles around us. We turn to science for fact to assimilate all around us into our own, created world. The problem is that we have the fallacy that the world is ours; that we control all. The problem with horse psychology is that we try to adapt it to our own knowledge of the world we want to create around us. We pretend to use studied basic instincts while often contradicting our own. If it seems confusing, a six-year-old child might give sound insight. Sometimes the answers are obvious, yet we refuse to see. That is where the complications come in.

This topic is not about wild horse herd behaviour. This is about the relationship between a human and a horse. The possibility already exists with any animal, and that includes people.

Talking to a horse is possible but does understanding take place? It certainly can. This is very real but in the context of being a human. Body language certainly works. Primarily, it is intent that is the main message in any situation. Intent or roles can switch between predator to predator, predator to prey, or prey to prey and even prey to predator. Maybe it would suffice to say that we are simply different species. I have seen horses strategically take turns to try to squash an aggressive dog like a fly, not run as prey from a predator even though they had the choice. We do not need to mimic horse aggression for a horse to know that we are angry or want him to move away or run. Likewise, being relaxed and inviting is not a replication of a mare allowing a horse back into a herd. It is simply being relaxed and inviting. No pretending. No façade.

We have journeyed on a linear path of control starting with the first club that smashed in another human's skull. Necessity is the mother of invention and we have made great advancements, mostly generated during warfare. Just because we can manipulate the world around us does not necessarily make us the wisest on the face of the planet. Sometimes, when we are looking for something specific, we are not always open to seeing what is really in front of us. When it comes to horses, and our quest for control, we tend to forget the simple power of love that we also possess. We are human and very slow and reluctant to change.

Reaching out to other species is far removed from scientific/psychological studies. We can analyze those to death, and varied conclusions may be reached according to what is being sought. Why? Because we are talking about horses. We are talking about the magic in our hearts, imagination, wonder, and beauty that has drawn us to horses for thousands of years. We also struggle with the notion for control.

The traditional tools for controlling a horse have not changed for thousands of years. However, towards the end of the 20th century, many new techniques surfaced that seemed less violent. It was more of a subtle, quiet violence. With joyous explanations and beautiful words or catch phrases, many new techniques were no less violent to the horse either physically or mentally. Actually, it was more of a combination of the two. They were just explained to us differently. Through the smooth method of modern marketing, many thought they had found the end of the rainbow.

I would briefly like to address two main training techniques. Although they are well known and have been analyzed over the years before, I still hear misinterpretations about them. They are from world-renowned trainers who created simple, systematic training methods that could easily be learned by people. The first is Parelli.[1] This technique breaks a horse in small stages that a person can easily learn. It is all negative reinforcement. That means do something uncomfortable to the horse until he responds appropriately. The horse is smart enough to quickly learn that he had better listen to the first request or else the subsequent orders will definitely get more severe. People could end up with a very quiet, obedient horse. It is that simple. No more, no less. Harmony has been created - for the human. Most people are very happy with that not realising that, for the horse, nothing has changed.

The second point comes from a very common phrase in the horse world. `A horse licking his lips is digesting the lesson`. This stems from the Join-Up from Monty Roberts.[2] To the human, seeing a horse do this is a good thing. It is, from that perspective, because the human has just won. However, the horse has just endured a mental/emotional trauma and the licking is an indicator of physiological stress relief. A blood test would show stress indicators through the roof. This method is also negative reinforcement, but is psychological. The horse does not even very well understand it. It can also inhibit future learning.

The idea behind the join-up is to replicate a mare expelling, for example, an unruly young horse to the outside of the herd. As a social animal, this is distressing for the horse who also relies on being part of the herd for protection. When the expelled horse agrees to be obedient or compliant, the mare will turn slightly away to indicate her acceptance of letting the horse back into the herd. However, our version of the process is in an enclosed ring. There is no escape for the horse. The horse is made to run in circles and change direction from an aggressor until the lowered head and lip licking gives the sign of submission from the horse.

These methods were very popular, and with most horses, they certainly work, and continue today. However, what I want to emphasize is the human interpretation of what is going on that is quite different from reality. Once again, nothing has really changed for the horse and most people do begin to see that somewhere down the line.

I tried Parelli, but did not get very thorough just with the seven games. I understood it, but just did not want to go down that road. Next up was the join-up. At first, I thought it was great. My poor Big Leo went through it all. I noticed Leo's confusion and something seriously wrong going on when I tried to apply it to some of those rejected horses sent to me in final desperation. All the nice explanations I had heard about what is supposedly going on in the horse during the join-up process, disappeared when I saw the physical reaction and expression from some of those horses. It still worked, to a degree, but without knowing exactly why the horses gave those expressions, I decided to drop that method, too. I started to learn that I had to stop seeking tools to put into my training bag. I was doing much better with horses when I knew nothing.

I do not want to go too much into science here, but for the lip licking, I feel it is important to make the differentiation about what is really going on in the horse. It is not the abounding belief that a horse is thinking and learning. Nevertheless, with this type of negative reinforcement the horse does learn how to quickly comply in order to make it stop.

Dr. Ian Weaver, of the Developmental and Stem Cell Biology Program, Toronto, Canada, continues studies relating to genome expression, how environmental factors can affect stress response and how it relates to the brain.[3] His work goes far beyond the basic physiological stress response as described here.

When dealing with stress the body reacts with increased heart rate, blood pressure and cells become metabolically active. Very young horses have legs almost as tall as the mature horses in order to keep up with the herd in a flight situation. The two main reactions in animals is the commonly known fight or flight. How they deal with stress is established at a very young age by the maternal presence and grooming. Those with higher contact or grooming physically better developed the ability to deal with stress.[4]

Stress hormones are produced during times of stress and are processed by the brain by one of the brain's major receptors, the glucocorticoid receptor. The ability of this receptor to remove corticosteroids, one of the stress hormones, assists in dealing with the stress response. However, if there are not enough receptors, the hormones remain in circulation thereby maintaining the elevated stress level. This reaction is useful for dangerous situations; however, prolonged or repeated increases in stress hormones can damage brain cells and impede thinking ability.

Cortisol (also known as hydrocortisone), a hormone produced by the adrenal gland, is the body's natural glucocorticoid. It has widespread effects throughout the body, increasing glucose production in the liver and promoting the breakdown of fat and protein. It causes sodium and fluid retention and potassium excretion, and inhibits the absorption of calcium from the intestines.

There was an article in Cavallo magazine, December 2003, which gave similar explanations and reversing the widely held belief about lip licking by:

Dr. Barbara Schöning, *Specialist in Animal Behaviour from Hamburg, Germany*

Dr. Sue McDonnell, *PhD in psychology and physiology and is Head of the Equine Behaviour Lab at the University of Pennsylvania.*

Dr. Francis Burton, *Brain Researcher and Behaviourist at the Institute of Biomedical & Life Sciences of the Scottish University of Glasgow.*

Lesley Skipper, *Equestrian author from the USA. Author of the book "Inside your horse's mind - A Study of Equine Intelligence and Human Prejudice".*

Mary Ann Simonds, *Wildlife and Range Ecologist, Equine Behaviourist and Therapist.*

Dr. Dirk Lebelt, *Specialist for Animal Behaviour at the Horse Clinic, Havelland in Brielow/Brandenburg, Germany.*

Andy Beck *from the "White Horse Farm Equine Ethology Project" in Northland/New Zealand studies equine behaviour and training methods on Thoroughbreds and Arabs.*

Professor Katherine Houpt, *Behavioural Psychologist and Physiologist at the College of Veterinary Behaviourists, Cornell University, Ithaca, NY, USA.*

Dr. Natalie Waran, *Expert for Equine Behaviour at the Royal School of Veterinary Sciences of the Scottish University of Edinburgh.*

Dr. Sharon Cregier, *Equine Ethologist, former Lecturer at the Canadian University of Prince Edward Island.*

Dr. Willa Bohnet, *Biologist and Expert for Equine Behaviour at the Center for Animal Welfare, School of Veterinary Medicine Hannover, Germany.*

Dr. Evelyn Hanggi, *Equine Behaviourist and President of the Equine Research Foundation in Aptos, California.*

Dr. Marthe Kiley-Worthington *from the Eco Research &*

Education Centre in Devon, UK, is the Grande dame of Animal Behaviour Research and she founded in 1959 the Research Stud Druimghiga.
Andrew McLean, *founder of the biggest Centre for Equine Behaviour in Australia, and member of the International Society of Applied Ethology.*

They all explained, in different ways, the basic result arising from the stress situation and how it affects horses physiologically and psychologically. Although I cannot find Cavallo today, through an internet search the full article can be found on some forums.

This is not about what is considered right or wrong. The truth will be accepted, rejected, or modified based mainly on what is suitable by humans and suits many different needs in just as many circumstances. Although scientific studies revealing the interpretation vs. reality of what we live with horses is valid, I will steer away from these types of examples. The reason is that such studies focus and dissect, in minute detail, biological and neurological responses. Often, but not always, they are still tainted with the notion of how this applies to training a horse with the biased human perspective. This is not exactly the direction that I wanted to go with my own horse. Although we are all biological, I also do not think that it is a direction that I would like to follow, hypothetically, in developing a relationship with my three-year-old daughter. Although understanding our inner processes can help to fight illness or disease, it is love, caring and nurturing that produces my desired results.

This brings to light an important distinction. We, as a

biological species like any other, still view other species as below us. This is not surprising because even in our endeavours to protect our own species, in reality, we also slaughter each other with abandon. Analyzing desensitization or behaviour is no different concerning horses as it is for us. In-depth analysis of simple interactions only reminds me of a manual for a new washing machine that may have three pages dedicated to how to switch it on. Merely the words `behaviour modification` categorizes and separates us from a true relationship with horses.

A Slap in the Face

I can give you a perfect example of all mentioned above. The very last time I used the round pen technique, or join-up, was in giving a demonstration to a student with one of my own horses. To protect a new horse that I may have in for temporary training from the rest of our herd, I had built a small round pen as an enclosure. I had explained the popular belief to a student and decided to show the process. The horse I was going to use was the youngest in our small herd. We were together since he was only four months old. The only method I used with him was to be caring, protective and to investigate the world around us. I acted with him as I would with a young child that did not speak English, or how a young boy would go out on daily adventures with a puppy.

We went into the round pen and he was staying with me, following me around, as he always naturally did. However, to demonstrate the procedure, I had to chase him away. Of course, it was not easy. He did not understand why I would do that. I noticed, but I was trying to make a point and I took his cooperation for granted. How foolish of me to slip back into any semblance of the norm. It was not a full-blown join-up session. The intention was to give a visual example of the procedure. The routine was short and condensed by asking the horse to change direction at about the halfway mark of the ring a couple of times. I did not push it to the point where the horse would finish by moving along with his nose to the ground. The example was simplified. The horse was not even running, although I still had difficulty in trying to keep the horse away from me to the fence line. My focus was mainly on the student while explaining the steps. Finally, as I turned slightly away and explained that the horse should come up behind me to my shoulder, the horse did come to me. It was not because of the process. That is what he wanted to do all along. As I was saying to the student, who was looking on, how the horse should now follow me around the pen, this young horse, which was never violent in any way toward me, did follow me for a few steps, and then left his teeth marks in the center of my back. I turned and saw his expression. His expression was the same as mine: Shocked, angry and confused. I was more so at myself than at the horse. That was the final realization for me about *pitfalls of following widely held beliefs while ignoring my own feelings*.

Two days later, after I had thought about all this and stopped kicking myself, I told the student what I believed really transpired in that round pen. I felt that it was important to tell her that I had made a very big mistake and the horse was quite right in being confused and upset. If I wanted to explain it to her, I should have found an existing video to show her instead. She was appreciative of my honesty. Because she did not have all kinds of methods or prescribed ideas in her head about horses, she understood. He bit me as if to say, 'Why the hell did you do that for?' I did not need a neuroscience study to help me understand that I betrayed my friend, the horse. His bite was as shocking to me as what he felt I did to him. The article from Cavallo is from 2003. I am writing this in 2010 and the reason is that I could still have someone wagging a finger in my face, arguing that my view of the join-up is wrong. What I had created with just a semblance of the join-up was a horse that many people would still say would benefit from the join-up! In reality, the horse did not change, but he definitely felt that I did.

As mentioned previously, the technique does often show results, but only if that is the type of relationship that you are looking for. One must realize that the role adopted is that of dictator. Aside from ignoring the inherent physiological, psychological and emotional problems, once you embark on that path, then you have to maintain the established hierarchy in all that you do with the horse. Most people like the idea presented behind that technique as a way of creating a bond with the horse. However, as we now know, it mostly causes confusion. It will serve to sever any honest interaction that may already exist. I believe that by adhering to that routine the horse comes to understand that you do not want a close friendship.

The relationship between that horse and me changed that day. It took time for us to come back to a trusting, understandable relationship. Actually, I should say, it took him almost a year to accept me with trust again. I had to prove myself a friend again. We were both not quite the same after that. Losing that initial relationship still weighs heavy on my heart. Yet, it remains an important lesson to me. Another very important lesson taught to me by a horse - because I finally listened directly to what I saw in the horse and not to a notion that was placed in my head.

In writing this book, so many different experiences have been relived and thought about. Why did I continue, for so long, still following outside norms of `training` a horse? Why did it take me so long to come to important conclusions? Did I not already realize that I was so much better with a horse when I knew nothing about `training` them? Old notions tend to cling to our minds like vines in an ancient forest. I had to stop looking outside for answers. Unless, I wanted to find justification to my own thoughts, such as contacting a neuroscientist.

There can be many metaphors to that bite in the back I received from that young horse. Ultimately, it helped close, at least, one door. In fact, it slammed it shut. Today, I do not need to adhere to any sort of conceived training. I do not need any kind of defence when talking to a local neighbour who only sees horses as a means of going trail riding, or a sportsman who will do almost anything to get into the next competition. It is not those activities of themselves but how the people view the horses. If I happen to bump into them and I am stuck in a conversation, I know that it is useless to try to convince these people about how I see things and what I have learned. I do not consider myself above them and I certainly have no fear of being persuaded to fall back into any old ways or in any other direction. We are on completely different paths for different reasons and different goals.

Horses have been my best teachers, and fortunately, somewhere along the way, I truly learned to listen instead of anticipating my own desired result. There is no turning back. It is that simple. It took many years and many horses to reach that simple realization. It took all that time and all those horses for me to overcome what people told me. I can only possess the certitude gained from those experiences by having gone through them. No amount of criticism or lecturing can replace what a person lives or will live. When I hear what others do to their horses and how they view them, I feel sad for their horses, and they think I am nuts because of what I do not do. In those cases, there is no immediate, fruitful discussion to be had between us at present. I might mention what I do, and very briefly explain why. Yet, in ten or twenty years, they may remember some of my comments about what I do and how I see things with my own horses. The reason why they reflect could come about from many circumstances. All of those reasons are painful. No one will listen unless he or she is ready to understand. They can only understand if they have lived the experience(s). It usually comes, sooner or later.

Self-Created Wall

A horse is large, heavy, and powerful. People can find ponies so cute, and yet be intimidated by a huge draft horse. In reality, such draft horses can have more tolerance and patience than a pony. It is not necessarily a rule, they all have different character, but it is important to note that image helps determine how most people will react. This is simply a fact from observation of people with different horses.

I have witnessed an interesting phenomenon with people and their horses. This may only apply to the West, where people have access to an abundance of horse information and training techniques. We are bombarded or surrounded by a plethora of ways to make this big, strong animal do what we want. It is so common, that we often do not see that the biggest horse can be as gentle, curious and willing as the smallest puppy.

It still surprises me when I meet people seeking a better way with horses and looking for a better relationship with them. They are often well educated about horses, in health, nutrition, homeopathy and massage techniques, try to give the best lifestyle for the horse as can be obtained in a domestic situation, and generally want the best for the horse. Yet, perhaps, as I experienced, many are stuck in some kind of norm of thought.

In many cases, such people are also vegetarian, or spiritual. They also have incredible relationships with dogs or birds. I have had people tell me about the characters, moods, of different animals in their lives. How they learned from each other, adapted to each other, learned likes and dislikes, to communicate fun, sadness, jealousy, curiosity, speech recognition and the simple processes of learning and growing together. In many cases, seeing this in action, I would directly ask the person why they called me. Why, after so many years of experience of relating to other species, did they not realise that they can simply do the same with horses? Why were horses inaccessibly beyond some imaginary curtain? It made many people think. However, it did not really change the situation.

If I had the power to take anyone's horse and shrink them down to the size of a Chihuahua, the relationship would instantly change between horse and owner. Mainly due to the person's new and different interaction with the super-mini horse, and more quality time spent with him. A lot more time. It would be so cuddly, loveable, and cute. They would laugh, stroke, tease, and play with the tiny horse. Just like, they do with dogs or cats or birds - but not with their real horse. Along with what we have been programmed to believe in the standard horse world, there is an aspect of fear involved.

Here is the story of two wolves from Cherokee wisdom:

One evening a Cherokee Elder told his grandson about a

battle that goes on inside people.

He said, "My son the battle is between two wolves inside us all. One is Evil. It is anger, envy, jealousy, sorrow, regret greed, arrogance, self-pity, guilt, resentment, inferiority, lies, false pride, superiority and ego.

The other is good. It is joy, peace, love, hope, serenity, humility, kindness, benevolence, empathy, generosity, truth, compassion and faith."

The grandson thought about it for a minute and then asked his grandfather, "Which wolf wins?"

The elder simply replied, "The one you feed."

We often try to ignore or suppress any negative feelings that we may have. Yet, we should try to understand those feelings and thoughts and accept them and deal with them. Allow the sum of our nature to bring forth something new and positive. Only then, can we develop, grow, and feel much freer.

At any stage along the development of the relationship with the horse, through the various interactions that we initiate or allow to evolve, we must be conscious of doing only that with which we are comfortable. Likewise, if we are very certain and emotionally comfortable about a particular request we may have, it does not automatically mean that the horse is at the same level. It is by being self-aware and by adjusting to the horse that we can progress through various comfort zones. This is not to say that a horse is harmless. Horses react to that which they are subjected. They are big, heavy and strong and a simple move from them can unintentionally, seriously injure us. Yet, it is simply abuse if we hammer repeatedly any reaction out of, or into, a horse. If we teach a horse, and I do not mean `train`, but really teach with patience and clarity for understanding, view the horse with a positive, creative, loving and happy attitude, then the self-imposed wall crumbles. Time spent with the horse should not be solely for trying to get something done. By treating the horse as a cherished companion, the barrier between human and horse ceases to exist. We will begin to see the gentleness, intelligence, and cooperation that were before us all along, but masked through proliferated notions that a horse is an animal that needs to be conquered and trained.

However, other impeding factors come into play regarding our relationship with horses. It is called daily life. I mean this in the context of standard society and all the pressures that come with modern life. We take it for granted as the norm, but it is not healthy for us, physically and mentally. It takes up the majority of our lives with forty or more hours per week. Many of us spend most of our time in an environment that is not natural for us. That is why a precious two-week vacation out of an entire year usually leads us to a tropical island or the seaside. It is like a return to our roots. That is if our jobs permit us the luxury of going beyond merely keeping up with costs or just surviving. Most of the time, we may have only a picture of clear blue skies, tropical forests, mountain ranges, or a seashore or wild horses on a calendar or computer screen saver.

Work affects us and drains us in more ways than we

may realise. Stress that begins just in the commute to work and poor diet contribute to the body drawing resources from itself or slowly breaking down and we are then ultimately subject to sickness, disease, lack of alertness and energy or depression. Most people who live this kind of `normal` life usually have their horse boarded somewhere because they certainly have no time in the day to look after all the needs of themselves, let alone, a horse.

Consider this: you may have adopted or bought a horse and you are the proud owner. Yet, the horse may not make such a connection because you are not the primary person in their life. The stable hand, or some other caretaker, is. You might say that it is your horse, but to the horse, you are a passing acquaintance. Are you someone who can pop in to visit for an hour in the evening? Is it maybe only on weekends? Are you always pressed for time? What do you do in that little time with the horse? Think about it.

The previous paragraph may hold true, but can also be quite different. For example, the horse is being trained. The primary person, who spends most time with the horse, is a trainer. If it is standard horse training, then that horse only knows that when that person shows up, it is the start of facing relentless demands. You, the stranger, with little time, little energy, and probably guilt, providing quiet time, grooming, carrots and attention can be quite a relief and pleasure for the horse. Who now becomes more important to the horse?

In any situation where we have a horse, we have to realise that they are captive. We need to consider what the horse needs from us. It would be like wanting to have a dog, but because you leave for work the dog is caged all day. If you do something like this, then it is seriously time to consider your own well-being. Something, somewhere, is obviously not right. We may have a desire that pulls us into a certain direction, despite our lifestyle, but we have to consider the well-being of any other living creature that we may bring into our lives, as well. By providing, caring, and sharing of ourselves, we can come closer to creating a new member of a family. That is the way it should be.

When boarding a horse, most establishments have their own standard of horse keeping and feeding. Different people working within that establishment or even other boarders may have different beliefs and methods of how a horse serves and how to handle the horse. Depending on the attitude of the people, the traffic in the place, and security, if any, has lead to some horses being improperly handled, ridden without permission or even abused, without the horse owner's knowledge, for the enjoyment or retribution of others. I have experienced our own horses suddenly develop behavioural anomalies: jumping at the sight of a broom, pulling in a panic on crossties, and refusal to enter a specific enclosure. A dramatic and fearful change in where there was no problem at all even just one day before. So many times I have heard the phrase from clients about a problem arising, '...all of a sudden', but I know that there were not any previous signs with my own horses. I soon found whip welts on the side of one of my horses, which was undeniable proof. One time, I caught a sweet-looking, pony-tailed, yet vindictive girl giving ten kilograms, or twenty-two pounds of sweet feed to our already labelled, so-called deadly Arabian mare. The reason behind that action was that she feared the horse and did not like having to share the arena for riding in the evening. Pump her with sugar and energy and we won't ride. I have heard of many similar, and worse, stories.

Going from visiting other people's horses, to renting out horses, to getting our own horses, it did not take very long to make the next step. The decision to leave the city was not only based on practicality, such as saving time and costs, but also the desire to be closer to the horses, to give them better lives, and, in turn, improve our own. Perhaps one of the main aspects about horses that draw us so intensely is their representation of the raw beauty and power of nature, and, their pure honesty. I love that honesty. When it comes to the elusive relationship that many seek with horses, part of the answer lies not in bringing them into our world by removing them from nature, but rather, in us returning to it. This does not mean to build a microcosm of human civilization in the middle of a forest, but to settle within the forest or countryside while creating as little environmental change around us as possible. In truth, our own journey should have been completely the opposite process by finding a place in the countryside, preparing it for horses, and then bring horses into our lives. Keeping it simple and in line with what a horse will be happier in, is much more cost effective! Do not make such a favourable change of getting your own place out in the country, yet still stick to the old ideals from life in the city by recreating the standard stabling life regarding horses!

None of what I have done with horses or how it affected our lives could have been foreseen. I have the good fortune that my wife loves nature and that we both had, and developed the same desires. It is easy for me to look back and see what could have been different, but it could not have been. It was a necessary path to follow to come to where we are today and to learn, from experiencing it, what I have learned. I wish that someone could have explained stuff like this to me a long time ago. It would have made sense to me even back then, as it probably would for any person who attains the long-desired dream of bringing a horse into his or her own life. In short, I have ended up where I wanted to start. There were just years in between where I was sidetracked by existing norms in the standard horse world, which is, really, a human world using horses. I have ended up with what I wanted, but I see things quite differently.

Horses really force us to be ourselves, or, to find ourselves. If we can simply let go of so much personal baggage, preconceived notions and expectations to be in the moment with the horse, we are usually amazed at the results.

I have seen a young child develop a better relationship with a horse than an educated adult. Horses may even offer a compromise or a solution to children when they figure out what a child may be trying to do. Could you imagine the sheer shock and, perhaps, jealousy from an adult upon seeing a horse lie down after a child is unsuccessfully trying to reach up in order to climb on? The same horse will willingly do more for the child than the adult who is trying to force a desired result.

Of course, we must have some kind of idea in mind when we go out to do something with horses, but as I have learned, the best method is no method. By this, I mean not calculated, presumed, assumed expectations geared towards training.

Our thoughts are extremely important because they are also directly linked to our body language and even our emotions. Ever hear the old phrase that `a horse can smell your fear`? If, as one example, Bach's Rescue Remedy reputedly works so well, it should not be too hard to believe that horses do pick up our pheromones. I have found that a horse ends up doing what we expect. Rather, what we truly feel deep inside is that to which they react.

One of my students once told me that her horse began to kick out at other horses when a few people were all riding in a group. Her horse had never kicked out at others before. However, on that particular day, she, the person, began to feel nervous about the other horses getting too close. In that case, the horse reacted exactly to how the rider thought and felt. I find that very interesting and will probably come as no surprise to many people out there. It is important to note that when the horse did react the way she expected or subconsciously wanted him to, that made her more nervous. She was afraid of losing control - of the horse. That is always the ultimate fear factor for riders. Here, she had such a connection with the horse and, yet, did not realize it, and was closing the door. Now, what did the horse have to go on? Now the person was very uncomfortable, did not want to be there, and wanted to get out of that situation. Take the horse's point of view. Was he not picking up more fear from the rider, tenseness, increased heart rate and increased or lowered breathing? All the signals both seen and unseen. The horse knows his reaction was not good enough and now, just on the surface, indications from the rider are getting worse. There must be some grave danger about, there must be monsters in the bushes, so maybe, with shared increasing stress levels, in uncertainty and confusion, it is time to completely get out of that situation and bolt? This is exactly what happened. The horse still physically did what the rider was thinking, but not in the exact way, that she was thinking it.

The most common attitude is that we want our young, green horses to be like an old cool-headed pro; we want our trained horse to be more like the refined winners; in often limited time we have available, we want our injured horse to perform anyway. We have to stay in the moment, second by second. Not only tell the horse, but also listen to the horse, and react accordingly. Most are disappointed and frustrated if the horse does not obtain an objective within one week or one month or even 30 minutes or 5 minutes, because we know what can be achieved down the road. We know what we want. However, are we really taking the time to teach or help the horse? Do we adjust to an action from the horse, or even consider what the horse is telling us? If we do not have time to communicate our intentions, how can we expect the horse to give us what we want anyway? It can always be forced, usually is, but I am not talking about that option. I think that should be clear by now.

Horses are not so much unlike us. So many horses bear hidden scars. If we get angry and frustrated in trying to do something with the horse, it is because the horses show us, directly, and that we are not doing the best we can do. I am certain that we have all had days where we have a lovely idea in mind and want the horse to do something, or rather, experience something together. Yet, it just is not working the way we planned. There have been days in the past where I just 'lost it' with my Big Leo. I had already lived and felt many indescribable experiences. I had seen the possible beauty but was seeking something that seemed elusive, and instead of feeling with love and patience, or changing my intentions by adapting to a situation, the same beauty I was seeking brought forth feelings of anger and frustration. It took a long time for me to realise that it was the angle that I was coming from emotionally that made all the difference. The horses had shown it to me when I least expected it. Therefore, I stopped expecting anything. That gave me everything.

It is not as simple as suddenly making a decision to change our apparent attitude. We can decide to change but only truly change when we come to some realizations. It is not so much that it is a work to build toward, but more important to let go of old thought and deal with feelings in a new way. It should be with love, or at least, honesty. The horses never changed. They were just waiting, patiently, for me to meet them halfway. They never forget, but they can forgive. If freedom, respect, understanding and teaching, is given to horses instead of trying to force them, they give us their all..

The First Hint

It was the middle of winter and I was leading a 3yr old, 15.3h (a hand is the measurement for the height of a horse from the ground to the highest point of the withers. A hand is four inches or 10.16 centimeters) Appaloosa up a road toward a forest where he would determine if he would let me get on him. Despite his size and build, three years old is still too young for riding. Although they can learn very well at a young age, the simple reason for not riding is due to lack of physical strength. Here is an important point and I will keep it very simple. Any of this information is available in books or any Google search from research centers to veterinary schools. This does not refer specifically to muscular strength, but bone growth. All horses have the same skeletal growth rate. Some may fully develop a little later, not because some horses develop faster, but because some breeds continue growing a little longer time. In short, the bone develops from the center of the bone toward the ends. A two-year-old horse has only developed partially solid bone from the hoof up to about the knee. As the growth continues upward and down the back, one of the last sections, but not the final development of the horse, is the spine. Unfortunately, the general norm, here in Quebec, and many other places, is not only introducing the saddle starting at two years old, but continued, prolonged riding/training from there. Early training and competition from young ages is what accounts for the breakdowns on the ever-popular racetrack. It is no wonder that micro fractures, multiple leg fractures and complete breaks are the norm. Even without the riding, there are the dangers that come with trying to get a horse to adjust to our mode of living. Such as the example of a horse pulling on crossties, or worse, being sacked out while on crossties or tied with a lead rope and halter to a post. As well as, lunging on small circles and always yanking the head into the circle. Again, great danger for the horse in what we consider perfectly normal training methods. The vertebrae at the base of the neck are the last to close fully. The earliest studies that I found, where I stopped looking, was a published article from 1953.[1] The horse industry is very well aware of the risks of riding young horses. They have commissioned some of the best scientific research. Why is the common horse owner unaware of these results?

In history, for military purposes, horses were never ridden before the age of four. Four years old is still not ideal to be plunged fully into service, yet better than today. Most horses are fully developed by age six. Not one certified trainer that I ever met ever mentioned anything close to this kind of information. Now, this important digression is really bare bones. Anyone can learn it in-depth, anywhere, if they look for it, or even honestly ask their vet... and get an honest answer.

The owner of the Appaloosa was afraid of the horse but wanted the gentlest training possible. Although it was understood that she would be riding the horse, she maintained a fear even though she witnessed me riding him. She did not even want to sit in the saddle with me holding the horse. A choice that was in direct conflict of her mother's wishes. Mother and daughter were polar opposites when it came to how a horse should be handled. Although I was not fully informed about growth process at the time, it was a dilemma for me to show the horse what would be expected of him because accepting a rider or not is what would determine his fate.

I used to describe what I called an imaginary line when leading a horse away from other horses and the stable. The horse can get increasingly expressive about going away from all the other horses, but there comes a point, a distance, where the horse was just in the moment with me. Behind is left behind. This brilliant horse, that most people considered `crazy`, was getting more tense and tried to contain himself as we got closer to that imaginary line, but suddenly veered and kicked out as we were walking along. I lost him.

I feared for his safety because of the closed reins dragging as he headed behind the stable with all kinds of farm equipment that might snag him. Moreover, if he went around to the front of the stable, I knew the reaction from people would be overkill. People would freak out at this `monster` being loose and make a simple situation an aberration. The horse would suffer even more by going back to what he thought was safety.

He galloped about two hundred feet, slowed and stopped. I had already started slowly walking back down the road but when he stopped and he turned halfway to me, I also stopped. I just signalled to him to come to me. I did not really expect that he would, but he did.

Although I was quite impressed with the horse when he decided to come back, it did not affect me the same way as that day on the trail where my life with horses forever changed. That will be covered later. Perhaps, because I may have been too focused on training, achieving a particular goal, that I did not fully benefit from that less dramatic experience. Looking back, two things were present in each case. First, there was emotion and second, the acceptance of the situation and not trying to catch the horse.

Being unable to catch the horse was what brought forth the emotion. I am not talking about anger or frustration about losing the horse. It was a swelling up and powerful projection of the danger that I visualized of the horse running on his current path and my intense desire that he not do so. In both those cases, the horse, which could have gone anywhere he wanted to, came back to me when I called his name and asked him, or even just signalled to come back. These were feelings not of demand, but necessity, even a desperate, emotionally felt, erupting plea. This was only my personal, culmination of my own thoughts and feelings. It was not any kind of intentional psychic call to the horse. It was merely my own, real reaction to the situation.

This is not really the direct result of a method, is it? I always told people that the greatest moments with our horses would be when there is no one around to witness or take a picture. Yet, the moment would be forever captured, and with time, our hearts will be filled with them. No best moments that happened with horses were because of an outward show of appearance, or some induced or forced reaction, but some kind of understanding, trust, and feeling that can go beyond words, beyond pictures, beyond the physical. Yet, it is merely two beings truthfully interacting.

Do not forget, however, that we are all biological. Feelings, and/or spirit, and biology are intertwined, or interfaced. Did the horses react to my emotion? Was it my thoughts? Perhaps it was a mix of both as seen through my entire body, face and eyes. Yet, in both cases, the horse was running *away* from me. They had already stopped and then turned to face me after the fact.

I pose those interesting questions to myself. However, I do not wish to concern myself with endless analysis. I have my answers to a certain degree. It is what is real in this world and in the unknown. I have experienced a connection in very real ways with horses. We are what we are, we live what we live, and we feel what we feel. Such is the world we live in. Here are real examples of the known mingled with the unknown. It all fell into place and, sometimes, not all is measurable by science and even it is, not fully understood. To me, thanks to the horses, this aspect of the intangible is no mystery. It is simple, it is honest, and it is beautiful. It is not something that we must seek, but is right before us. It has always been within us.

The Magical Forest

The stable where the Appaloosa was kept was large and with a clubhouse, had two round pens, a large sand-filled, outdoor riding ring and paddock areas in the back. I never liked working with a horse there when people could watch. If riding, I was not interested in going around in circles within one of the riding rings. Saddling up the horse and getting out of the stable was really an outing. We drifted further and further from the stable. A dirt road ran out behind the stable and rose up toward a forest about thirty minutes walk away. Pastures on either side provided both pleasure, leisure, and an exercise in focus if it was time to walk on the road. I always started out just leading a horse and about halfway up toward the forest, I would ask the horse to stop. He was groomed, saddled, walked with me and listened, so we stopped to have some time for what was most interesting to him. I could not release the horse, but we meandered about in the field. He grazed, I stroked him gently and scratched his withers and moved with him when he moved to a new spot. When I would ask him to get his head up and follow me, he did. They all did. Allowing a horse to eat or graze while under saddle is probably against standard beliefs, but I find that a little give and take for what we both wanted went a long way.

At the end of the slow incline, there is one last rise of about thirty degrees to get up to the forest. From there the view was impressive. We would also pause there to look out at the land and the sprawling developments beyond that stretched out before us. We felt the breeze, heard the birds behind us, and it was like being between earth and sky. We would then turn to continue on our way and were on the verge of the narrowing path to entering the forest.

When we would finally enter among the trees that was where we left everything behind. Only minutes away from the normal world, but it was like suddenly being alone, in peace, among the tranquil hush of nature. There were paths that branched out in different directions or crisscrossed along the way. We would follow connecting paths that simply formed a loop to bring us back to the forest entrance. This circuit could take only about twenty minutes to complete at walk and trot. In the summer, we immediately enjoyed the sudden coolness among the trees. However, this was winter. We still had the stillness with protection from wind or blowing snow. In this case, it kept us warmer.

I could be walking in powder snow that went up to about halfway between my ankle and knee. About one foot or thirty centimeters deep, more or less in areas, as long as we stayed on the path. While still leading the horse, I would ask for stops, turns, reassure, and I would talk, or sing quietly. At times, we would stop and just listen to the silence. After that, I would `hug` the horse with my arm over the saddle as we walked. I would watch him closely for his feeling about this. If it seemed fine, I would take the reins and mane in hand and place a foot in the stirrup. I would still watch him closely for his feeling about this. Every time I decided to do this is because it seemed like the right time. If the horse gave any look of merely a surprise in his eye, I would just reassure and we would continue walking together as I laughed and made no big deal of it. I had discovered that, as long as I really felt it, laughter dissipated a lot of anxiety in the horse almost instantly. I would soon try again. Most often, by the time I did this, the horse might turn and look at me and then stand straight again. Quiet, still, and calm. I would rise in the stirrup and still check for reaction and agreement and only then sit in the saddle, praise, reassure and then ask to walk. What happened was that as I finally went to mount, on my last spring, one of my legs sank into the snow. I ended up swinging in front of the horse's shoulder with my back against his neck. How graceful. I stepped down and laughed at myself. The horse did not freak out thinking that maybe I was assaulting him. The horse just looked at me and stood still. Once again, I went straight to the mounting, still smiling. The horse would carry me through the solitude of the forest, which held an ineffable beauty in the stillness of the snow covered trees. No stress, no panic, no fear. I did not jump on his back forcing him to accept. We walked together from the beginning and he could see that I was much more tired than he was. He knew what I wanted and he permitted me to ride him. Every time this happened, I gave thanks for this experience. It was no less beautiful every time. Then I would dismount and we would walk side by side once more. On the final stretch of the main road, I would mount and we built up to canter, and down to trot, walk, and stop. This was on the same road where he initially, desperately wanted to get back to the other horses. I would dismount and we would finish our walk as we started, but with an entirely new understanding between us.

I had picked up that tip from Xenophon, approximate birth date of 431 BC, who wrote the first book on `sympathetic` horsemanship.[1] He wrote that a rider should dismount one mile away when returning to the horse stable. The first time I tried this was upon returning from a trail ride with a rented horse. That initial phase of wanting to be with horses again was short-lived. It troubled me to see the overall state, physical and emotional, of those horses saddled and tied up all day long, except when strangers came along to make them do another shift of hard work. When I dismounted before getting back to the starting point, the horse looked at me with surprise, or maybe apprehension of the meaning of this different behaviour. It was not a mile away, but he gave a big sigh and relaxed as we walked on. I went to the rental place once more after that. When that horse saw me, his head came up from his slumber, he looked straight at me, and he nickered softly. He remembered me. If giving this horse a break, or showing a little courtesy seemed to make such a difference, then I began to feel guilty about riding him in the first place. I could not save him from his daily routine, and so I never returned after that. It still took more years, more horses, more hints, before I began to sway away even more from the ingrained thought in society as only seeing horses for riding.

With the experience of the young Appaloosa, that forest was magical because I thought of it as leaving the world behind. I felt that it was good for the horses for the same reason. However, the working horses there that were rented out for trail rides did not see the forest in the same way. They were often very reluctant when the stable hand went out to catch them in their enclosure. I could very well see that the horses knew what they would have to endure. Far too often, it was one hour or more of a stranger seeking personal enjoyment upon their battered backs, who only fearfully thought of maintaining control, jerking, yanking, or hanging on the reins connected to the metal in the horse's mouth. The only way most horses would walk back along that final stretch would be due to exhaustion or pain. Pain either developed, or induced or feared. These are facts seldom recognized or even vaguely thought about by `horse lovers`. That is where the previously mentioned one-sided fulfillment comes in. It is not necessarily a lack of sensitivity, but awareness could make a very big difference. What else do most people in the public know about horses other than getting on and riding?

Within this very story, am I being hypocritical? At the time, I loved riding, too. What kind of fulfillment can I claim the horse had by permitting me to ride? I can say only that, in my view, it did not bother him at that moment. I did not abuse the gift granted to me by the horse. It was based on respect and understanding. Recognizing what is acceptable to the horse, in real time, is very important. Just because I could ride him once, or several times, does not mean that, he is willing and ready every single time in the future. I have to recognize that and respect it. By doing so, he is willing when the time is right. Every time, just like the first, I always consider it a gift from the horse, not a duty.

It was these kinds of experiences with the horse, away from the standard norm, that allowed me to see a side of the horse that most people overlook. It is no wonder that I was an oddball in the horse world. It is no wonder, because of this, that I was the most successful with any horse in any stable. This was mostly, with horses that had been considered `rejects` or given up on.

For riders and non-riders alike, if I were to ask if the horse was created for riding, 99.9% of respondents would say, no. Yet, in reality, most people think, `What else is a horse for? `. The overwhelming consensus is that a horse is supposed to be used for something. In the general terms and in the standard horse world, our love for the horse only causes damage. Horses are very good at masking locomotor problems and humans are not so good at noticing. When there is a problem, we often do not think about what has caused it, but only seek a quick remedy. There are abundant ways to fix wounds, mask muscle trauma, soreness, lameness, in order to get the horse to walk out of his box the next day anyway. The horse may quietly go on and endure until one day he can no longer perform. That day is way short of his normal life. Because, when he can no longer perform, loving owners tearfully end his life. Alternatively, gracefully retire him and then, with a new horse, proceed to duplicate exactly what they have previously done. The numbers of horses that have been freely offered to me each month justify these statements. I am told that the horse `...can't keep up`, or has serious physical ailments impeding the human's goals of fun and/or competition. All caused by the singular ideas of why a horse exists.

When spring arrived that same year, the owner of the Appaloosa wanted me to continue to work with her horse. Although we had started in snow, most of that winter was mild with a lot of freezing rain. Ground conditions varied between mud, frozen ground or sheer ice. The snow in the forest had become too soft. When the weather was warming and the ground had dried up, we went back to the forest where leaves and flowers were budding anew.

We started following the same paths and did the same routine as we did on the finer winter days. When I mounted, in almost the same area as during the winter, the horse had no problem with this at all. I asked him to walk and stroked the side of his withers, telling him he was a good boy. We walked on loose rein and I noticed how he drifted to the side of the path smelling branches of leaves as we passed. That time of year is so pleasant. Warm, dry, with active animal life and flourishing plants and early enough that there are no flies or mosquitoes. He walked calmly and relaxed with his neck slightly below horizontal and as we passed a bush with fresh flowers, he closed his eyes and stroked his face alongside them. I think my mouth fell open and my heart swelled. In that small moment, I realized that he had lived the standard, domesticated horse life from the very beginning. Our outings and this spring bloom were the only times he had encountered nature. Being on a cleared path, surrounded by sheltering trees in the winter was one thing, but this was entirely new for him and he obviously loved it. He was exploring the scents, seeing, and feeling flowers for the first time.

It made me realize how much I take for granted and overlook in daily life, even in what I considered our private paradise. It reminded me again of the reality that most horses live despite the different feelings that may attract us to them in the first place. I dismounted and we went back to the bushes and flowers. I had never done something like that before and I had no real plan or expectation of what would come of it. He had been doing for me what he figured I wanted. I felt that, by letting me ride, after building a relationship and the way we worked together, this horse was showing courtesy and kindness, not submission to a human master. When we stopped and he knew that I noticed what he did, his eyes lit up. He seemed like a child that was granted a day in Disney Land when we went back to the flowers. I was actively thinking about the importance of being in nature, yet, being familiar with that path through the forest, it became routine. There I believed that I was spending time among the vibrant beauty while I was passing it by most of the time. Looking but not seeing. We went off to explore a completely new world off the beaten path... with me on foot.

It is a day that I shall never forget. This horse had helped me to clarify and crystallize my own feelings and view of what a relationship with a horse could be - should be. I had been on a distant, parallel path of standard horse training. That horse, that day, pulled the intellectual veil away from it. Pulled me closer to him and allowed my true voice from within to surface.

The owner noticed how we were never around the stable for training. In her weekly visit, we met her walking up the road that leads to the forest. We trotted up to her and stopped. After all this time, she was still surprised at how her horse listened so well without a bit. She asked me if I would be willing to board this horse at my place to complete training. That was the sweet icing on a perfect day.

A Brief Respite

I transported that horse to our place myself. Compared to where he came from, including the attitudes toward him, our open, green spaces and lines of pine trees was like Club Med for him. He and our horses adjusted quickly to each other and he was right at home in no time. The problem was that this was not his real home.

We are not high in the sky like the magical forest, and the ground was still very soft at home. With any spring rains, we were just waterlogged or in mud again. We could only walk in-hand along the gravel part of the driveway that extended into the field and practiced hoof cleaning and trimming. Although that was important, so was the time he simply was allowed to be a horse with other horses.

On a warm Sunday, the mother and daughter visited our place. We stood by the fence to the paddock and watched the horse role in the driest spot available. The mother asked the daughter if she wanted to ride, and her answer was still no. She asked me if I had ridden the horse lately, and with the obvious ground condition around us, I told her no. Within that same week, the mother had decided to pull the horse out and send him to her training stable that specialized in racehorses.

They showed up with their own transport and the man could not get the horse into the trailer. Not even close to it. Before things got worse, I stepped up and said that the horse was accustomed to me, so I should try leading him in. I reassured the big boy and we walked calmly, straight into the trailer. The girl was shocked. She could not comprehend how I did that because, she said, the transporter had twenty-five years experience. She could not believe that we just walked into the trailer.

Once inside, the horse and I had a moment alone. I knew this was the end and as I was tying him to the front of the trailer, I thanked him for being my friend and even explained that he was now going back with the girl. He stood still and listened. I gently stroked his face with love and he lowered his head and put his forehead against my chest. He seemed to know what was happening or at least sensed my own feelings. I do not think he would have let anyone else get him into that trailer. I felt that it was his last gift to me. It is as if we were both numbly resigned to the fact that our time together was over. I stepped out the side door and told the girl that they should close up the trailer and head out right away. The young woman was still standing there with a look of wonderment, jaw dropped, arms down and palms forward with fingers outstretched. I walked away into the field trying to contain my sadness, helplessness and tears. I could not look back.

The Three Horses

Slowly, I began to realize that if what I was doing with horses was working, then it was of paramount importance that the owners understood, believed in, and actively wanted to learn the same fundamentals. Although I had developed my ideals, I was still naïve in the sense that I took people's word, or most of what they said as what they truly believed in or desired. I had a tendency of focusing only on the aspect that pertained to what I liked to hear. Perhaps, I automatically assumed that what I heard on the surface meant the same as my own deeper understanding. Humans are often not honest, mostly with themselves. I always look for the good in people, but they are certainly not clear and direct like horses. I had to understand that if people thought and did exactly as I did with horses, they would not be asking for my help. This was the case where I had two months to get three horses ground trained for handling, saddle trained, trail trained, and being like smooth, experienced, rock solid, bombproof horses for completely new, inexperienced owners.

It is when that last part finally sank in that I realized I had quite a challenge. It was October and the owner told me that he, his wife, and daughter wanted to ride those horses by Christmas. If you noticed, the clock was ticking...

Here is where a Canadian horse came into my life. A six-year-old mare and she was stunning and as expressive as an Arabian was. She had character and an opinion and let it show. She was supposedly trained as a sleigh horse. I know that she came with a higher than usual price tag than most rejected horses did. Nevertheless, she did not want to know anything about equipment. The Canadian, the thirteen-year-old Paint mare, hardly ever handled, but used for breeding, and the seven-year-old black and white Paint, put through the mill and then rejected, were all very wary of humans. They all had different pasts, but these great horses were being sold second-hand for the same reason.

I knew that with all three horses, all was possible, in a positive way. They were all intelligent and at least willing to listen. Only the black and white Paint had endured, I am certain, a very hard training in the past. He was the only one that was saddle broke, but very reluctant. I had to start over with everything.

I recall mostly the first meeting with the black and white Paint. He was distant and turned away when I entered his box at the reseller. I stood at the door and only tried to express that this was his last chance. I could help him or try my best. He would turn his head, look at me, and turn away again to face the corner. I do not know what he went through, but I could be sure that it was hard on him. I felt that he was resigned and ready to die rather than to try again with another person. Given my choice, he said no. When the reseller finally grabbed him, when he arrived, he did not put up a fight. This horse was obedient, but void.

I knew if given a chance and showed real proof of what I felt that I had to offer, life and light could return to his eyes. I was already on this road and I wanted him to give me that chance. It was as much for his sake as for mine.

The other mare, a Paint, was almost like a Palomino and with one blue eye. She was smart, and I recall when I first tried to lunge her and raised the lunge whip, she stopped, faced me and visibly shook in fear. I threw away the whip. At thirteen years old, she was afraid of people, always seeming to expect something bad to happen. She had little experience with anything because she had been used for breeding only. It took time to gain confidence, and at least, by the deadline, Christmas, we were able to take a walk, the whole family, riding those three horses, through a fresh, snowy trail as I lead the way on foot. I felt that the horses would feel more at ease this way because that is how I started with them, and they knew what to expect.

The Canadian mare was also very wary of humans. She expected force and violence and was on guard to react against it with force. She was also very intelligent and learned that I asked for very simple things and gave her the choice. For the saddle and start of riding, I did it in small segments. If she accepted the saddle on her back for a moment, I would remove it and stop there. She started to give me subtle signals when she would become uncertain. I never pushed it with her and by doing so, she was willing to listen further and discover what I was trying to do.

Within two days, of sessions not more than twenty minutes each, I could sit in the saddle on her. I did not want to lose her confidence, so even to walk forward we followed the same type of learning. I did not just want to get her going under saddle without her understanding what we were doing. I placed two orange cones, similar to traffic cones, about fifteen feet apart. I would point to the cone, say, `cone` and lead her over to it. It did not take long for her to walk to it on her own while I stood still. When she was quite comfortable with this new game, I mounted, said, `cone` and she walked over to it. Two well understood exercises put together. I would then immediately dismount. Each day, I would add more distance between the cones and then added a third to form an L-shape, and then a fourth to make a square. Constant reassurance and praise after completing a designated task further showed her that I was not like the others she may have known. This became so clear to her that I felt that she enjoyed being able to show me how capable and smart she was. If I sent her off on her own, she would complete the circuit. We each listened and learned from each other. From doing this on the ground, and then to saddle, we walked a square within the riding ring by the end of one week.

I had shown her that to walk to that cone was simple and non-threatening. It all worked and that helped her focus and helped us gain confidence together and be able to continue without fear or apprehension. This went both ways, for I did not know what kind of life through which she had really been. With her strong character, I quickly learned that it was the way that I asked that made all the difference for her. You must have heard the old saying, ask a mare, tell a gelding, discuss with a stallion... well, I discussed and asked with all horses and it always worked. Eventually, I was riding her while ponying the black and white Paint. She helped me by helping the Paint understand to keep pace and not bolt off. It is as if she understood what we were trying to do and did not just follow my commands by carrying me around, but she took an active role in teaching.

A brief story about another horse, at another time, that helped me with teaching. A previous owner had tried to train the horse to pull a sleigh. There was not much preparation for the horse to accept or understand any of what he was expected to do. He was put in a harness, hooked up to a sleigh and driven forward. The horse was terrified and afraid of just the sight of a sleigh. I managed to help him with that just because they are so common in our province, but my task was to train him under saddle to be sold as a trail horse. That horse did great and we could not only ride trails, but also do obstacle courses. After the training, the owner successfully sold the horse, but the new owner became afraid to ride because the horse would often just run out of control. I discovered this because the new owner asked me to saddle train another horse that was also recently purchased and after hearing about the difficulty of riding the horse that I knew, I decided to give it a go.

Saddling up the horse I had previously trained was no problem and mounting was no problem, but just starting to walk, I noticed that the horse was getting uptight. I just reassured him saying, 'easy' and 'it's okay', stroked his neck, visualized just walking around the outdoor enclosure. The horse calmed down and carried me with no problem. Did he just need reassurance?

We did not have much room to work in, and after introducing the saddle to the new horse, I wanted to help the horse understand, through observation, what was expected of her. I preferred to pony the horse rather than trying to desensitize the horse to the feeling and movement of the saddle through lunging. That was the most common technique that I usually witnessed, and the horse usually panics and bucks while the person keeps driving the horse, yanking the head into the circle. They keep up that type of training until the horse is no longer bothered or afraid of the saddle and the flapping of the stirrups, or eventually just gives up by being resigned to the fact that it must be accepted because there is no escape.

After presenting a saddle to the new horse, I made contact with it in stages, or parts, by first just using a blanket, then adding a surcingle, then the saddle alone, then cinching up, then adding the stirrups. While in hand, stationary, I would squeeze across the top of the saddle, put pressure on the stirrup straps, slide and bump the stirrups along the side of the horse, walk in hand. All this was well understood with no fuss and no fear. The horse that accepted me as a rider was going to help me to further the task. It was obvious that he felt useful when we started this. A slight uncertainty at the very beginning quickly changed to understanding that we were teaching the other horse and a sense of purpose showed in his behaviour.

This horse showed me that he was happy to be doing something and to be counted on by me. He wanted to be useful. When I would show up for another training session, I first placed the two saddles on the fence, and went to groom the new horse. I heard something and when I turned around my 'assistant' had placed his nose under a saddle and was trying to toss it up over his head and neck. He was trying to get the saddle on himself and trying to tell me that he wanted in on this session. He then did that every time that I went there. I would watch him and he was not just sniffing or chewing at the saddle, it was an obvious, deliberate attempt to slide under the saddle. The closest he got in his attempts was to get the saddle up, through small nudges, straddled across his face and bumped up to the top of his head like a hat and then it would tip over to the ground. I definitely would have to have seen it to believe it.

The owner of the Canadian mare really seemed to understand where I was coming from and he did get along well with her. She accepted him. He was *her* rider. We had rode out together in late winter, in unpredictable conditions, he with the mare and I with the black and white Paint. It was an adventure. There were trees down, rushing water of streams from melting snow heading down toward the slopes, soft snow, mud, and all the winter debris from trees among the forest floor. At one point, from the corner of my eye, I saw the mare's head at just above the level of snow. I stopped, dismounted, and saw that she had not fallen, but sank with all four legs straight down into the soft shoulder of the snowy trail. The owner just rolled off the saddle to the side. The mare removed her front legs from the soft snow, pulled herself forward, and up by herself. She was calm, shook off the snow and was ready to go. The man mounted again and we continued on, knowing to stay more in the center of the trail. We got lost at one point when I took a wrong turn within barely visible forest trail where there was no snow. I had only been there the previous spring. We were walking about in sparse forest with no way of really knowing where we were going. Somehow, we found our way back and that way was by letting the horse choose which direction to go when I was undecided. I had noticed that the horse had wanted to take a turn at one point on our way in. The second time, I followed his advice.

I have heard of stories from people who would lose track of time while out riding, lose their way, to end up in darkness after sunset. Knowing that they were utterly lost, they would drop the reins and ask the horse to take them home.

We came to a temporary rushing stream of snow run-off. The Paint was hesitant to cross, so the owner of the Canadian, sensing his own horse and with confidence, did not hesitate, and asked us to step aside so that they could cross. They took the lead and it gave the Paint the confidence to follow the example. Crossing such streams, small or large, was no longer a problem. The Paint was always considered unpredictable and would just tense up and gallop off with the owner. That was his only `problem`. He was not unstoppable, but I believe he was previously trained to go full tilt at the slightest indication. All I did was allow him to relax and let him know that walking was fine. He understood and was no longer a live wire. I sensed that he seemed relieved by it. He was cool headed, responsive and an integral part of our lost adventure.

When we got back to the stable, the owner of the black and white Paint asked how it went. Her husband, beaming from the saddle of the Canadian, smiled and said, `There is nothing wrong with your horse. It must be you...` He said it almost jokingly to her, but I saw the quick reaction on the woman's face. It was an inner reflection receding deep behind her eyes. She did not ask what he meant, or for any kind of explanation, or what occurred on the trail. That comment ripped a piece of her away. The final piece. Not being able to ride her horse made her feel progressively unconfident in herself. Instead of happiness, she felt fear and frustration. She wanted to live the experience we had just been on, but would never dare to venture out as we just did.

There were, of course, great moments between those horses and the owners. Especially the first day that they were able to mount their own horses and ride on a lunge line. Smiles, photos, sheer happiness and hope. The teenage girl, who was apprehensive about riding the Paint with the blue eye, surprised me one day by asking if she could take her horse to go ride on trail with another girl from the stable. By that time, I knew the horse was ready and capable, and now it seemed the girl was, too. They had walked, trotted and cantered. She had a fabulous time and I later received a phone call from the mother explaining that to me. Her daughter had spent a day floating on cloud nine. However, weeks later, on a very warm, sunny day signalling the real advent of the end of winter, she fell from the horse in the riding ring.

The place was very busy because of the beautiful, first Spring-like day. There were riders in and out of the ring, vehicles coming and going, children laughing and playing in the piled snow around the ring, dogs running about. The mare was in heat and all the commotion that she was rarely exposed to previously, was a little too much for her. I could see her tension rising. Still, she was controlling herself, and I decided to end the riding lesson in the ring and take it outside the ring away from the busy stable.

I asked the girl to make one final pass to grasp a tennis ball that I had placed atop a thin metal rod earlier in the day just near the gate to the ring. This rod was held vertical by being placed in the center of an orange cone. Unfortunately, I had not noticed that someone jammed the metal rod into the ball. It was no longer loose to fall off the rod if she missed, or to come off if she grabbed it. She, and the horse, was good enough to be able to pass close at trot and grasp the ball. The rod, firmly attached to the ball, came up out of the cone as the girl grasped the ball in her hand. As they passed the cone, with the momentum, the rod swung forward beside the horse's head. A thin rod was suddenly swinging beside the face of this tense horse that was already fearful of whips. She got surprised, stopped and gave a few small stationary bucks and the girl fell into the sand. She suffered a sprained wrist but the greatest injury was not physical, for both the girl and the horse.

After bringing the girl, who was in tears, inside to her mother, I returned to the mare. She was visibly angry and not very agreeable, but not violent. She felt betrayed. She was uncooperative and pouting. When I mounted and asked her to walk, she was defiant. She would resist a rein, toss her head, gave small bucks. She wanted me to get off of her. That may sound like a lot of different emotions and reactions from a horse but that is what I saw and clearly understood. I lead her away from the stable up the quiet road that stretched behind it. I reassured her, and we walked together and she calmed down. It was a huge relief for her. Yet, in her eyes I swear I could see, 'Oh no, what did I do back there? '. I quietly rode her back to the stable with no further trouble. I do not think that neither the girl, nor the parents fully understood that it was the swinging rod that spooked the horse. I believe that, despite my explanations, they thought the horse had changed and was now dangerous.

All these events were very close together, but now mother and daughter were not riding their own horses. From the look on the woman's face after the comment from her husband about her being the problem, not the horse, without another word, I knew it was over for me. She was going to find another way or another person to make her dream happen for her. The same week, I saw the horses go into the hands of an older trainer who promptly replaced the bitless bridles with bitted ones and would punch, kick or beat the horse about the head to punish them while riding. That is exactly what these horses could not tolerate. They fought in defiance and outrage, yet, I saw the light disappear from their eyes once again. They stood in their boxes motionless, looking exhausted, dejected and confused. Looking at the Canadian, who seemed so uncertain now, through the bars of the box, made me think of that horse I came so close to buying years before. I could no longer bear to go to that stable anymore. I later heard that all three horses were, one by one, once again rejected, being deemed unrideable or dangerous. They were sent away and soon replaced with old, experienced Quarter Horses that were chosen for the owners. That is a good choice for new riders whose focus is on their own riding. It is not what I solely believed that family initially wanted. With the passage of time, I hope that they could recall the great moments they had with those first horses; the boundaries they were able to cross within themselves and with the horses.

I never learned the true fate of those three horses. I can only hope that they did not have to endure several repetitions of being bought and sold with attempts by several new owners to train them into `good` horses. I hope none of them ended up on a grocery store shelf. I hope that people with patience and understanding to see what those horses could really give, if given respect and the chance, provided a happy life for them.

The Night-Mare

"There are so many good horses out there. Why waste your time with this one?"

That sums up what we often heard about Phantom. She is a grey, Polish Arabian mare. She was a dancer, a prancer, a rearer, a biter, a kicker. It was not so when we brought her to the first stable at which she was boarded. Of course, she was still under two years old, could be haltered and led, but she was far from calm. She hated being in a box. She was a normal, young horse full of energy. She required communication to understand what we were going to do, even if it was to explore around the barn. My wife had started doing this and I have to admit that, at the time, I found her approach childlike. She could talk up a storm with Phantom by describing what they were going to do and explaining about things. It appeared to me like too much talk and not enough action. It was not exactly the same way that I did things. I was more physically reassuring, observant, and quiet. Yet, she got the horse through some strange experiences where, if Phantom were alone, it would be an instant flee situation, if she even dared to advance to that point at all. It could be something simple like walking through a very dark alley and encountering a chair, analyzing it, and moving on. She needed reassurance, time to absorb any new sight or task without being forced onward and mostly confidence, gentleness and calmness from us. She needed to be asked, not told, what to do and she needed to know why. Much of her demonstrated frustration came from her wanting to be heard and understood. We had no problem with her. She was a nightmare for anyone else who would impose themselves while taking for granted that she was just any 'shut up and listen' horse. If I found Monica's approach childlike, then it should come as no surprise that Phantom would nod 'yes' or tilt her head from side to side as a 'no' when she asked if she was comfortable with something. The 'yes' movement was calm and the 'no' showed that she was evidently upset. Monica taught her that and Phantom used it.

Although I did not realize it at the time, Phantom's character and intelligence helped me to learn to teach. I mean really to teach a horse by reaching out; finding ways to explain to achieve comprehension and to witness the student go from an apprehensive blank to thinking and understanding. It was not training in the typical sense. Certainly not action-reaction based solely on outward physical threats or fear from a whip or any other type of aggression commonly used in standard horse training. Nevertheless, I still followed common routines like lunging or long reining and getting her to do all the other stuff that a horse is expected to do in a regular stable. I can write this comparison or explanation now, but at the time, foregoing what we saw in videos or books seemed the natural way to proceed with her. Volumes of training videos and books piled up and gathered dust because the solution to how to handle her and teach her was right in front of us. She was right in front of us clearly showing us what the problem was and how to overcome it. It had to be a partnership, a respectful exchange of intent, thought and ability to learn about and adjust to *each other*.

At times, even in her expressive reluctance or frustration, if I maintained a communication with her and reassurance, she would try to focus again. It was moment by moment, and I had to learn to be patient and adjust every time she would say that she did not want to continue or was scared or frustrated due to lack of understanding. She continually forced me to find ways to help her understand.

In the introduction to this book, I mentioned the importance of recognizing our true feelings based on what we actually see and drawing forth from the wellspring of our own experiences. Moreover, to have faith in those feelings and ourselves even if they are not always in accordance with a particular standard norm. As simple as this seems, it can be a little tricky, for we sometimes can reach quick conclusions about what we perceive and do so with absolute certainty. At times, even with our best intentions in mind, we can carry many different assumptions and even prejudice toward any particular horse.

Any horse owner that keeps a horse at home knows that it is a like a full-time job, or at least, like being on call 24/7 and vacations are, most likely, less likely. There was one time that we planned to get away for the weekend and this was possible because my mother was going to stay to care for the horses for us. She was not really a horse person, other than the fact that she was born in the '30s and when she was growing up, horses were still part of the workforce in society. Like many families during her generation, backyard stables were common in the city, but it was the last leg of horses pulling carts, dirt roads, Sunday carriage rides along cow fields. It was the dawn of the modern metropolis. Streets were being paved for automobiles and city expansion and development saw the disappearance of expansive fields and cow crossings within city limits.

It was during late summer and while we were away, Phantom, the very expressive and intelligent Arabian mare, was pawing at the newly installed water line that was exposed above ground near the house. The water line fed an outdoor drinking fountain for the horses. In doing so, she caused a joint in the hose to come undone and the water gushed from the opening. My mother later explained to us that she saw Phantom doing this and her opinion was that it was intentional and malicious. She believed that the horse broke the water line on purpose. From her experience of how horses should be, any horse that did anything but stand still waiting for a command to work was being a bad horse.

How do I describe Phantom? Intelligent and expressive. She pawed at that hose for a reason. I think I know the reason and it was indeed deliberate. The horses are loose outside and, although they could go into the barn to drink, they usually preferred to access the water outside in the shade of the trees. It was more convenient. An oversight, on my part, was to forget to explain to my mother that the exposed water line, sitting idle in the sun, created very hot water in the hose. It had to be checked and possibly run periodically so that the water was cool and fresh to the outside fountain. She saw a bad horse, but I saw a horse that was smart enough to say, 'Hey! Check this! It's no good!' and she kept at it, trying to send that message, until the hose gave way. Understandably, my mother did not hear that message at all.

Some of the students that took lessons with us at home were able to work with Phantom. The ones who were able to do this had to have a sense of confidence in themselves and an open respect toward the horse. They had to understand how I described the horses to them and be able to adjust accordingly to different reactions. In other words, the ones who understood me and listened to the horses were successful.

Phantom would start to get nervous if someone just put a halter on her, clipped on a lead line, and started walking. That never changed with her. It was not a matter of habituation through repetition. It seems strange, but she would be better if she were told that she was going to be saddled, lead out, and take a rider around our land. When I wanted to teach a twelve-year-old girl how to lunge a horse, there was one horse, Peppy, that, if I were present, would respond perfectly with anyone almost every time. I wanted the girl to learn how to interact with a horse and not just stand still while a horse went around her in circles. Phantom was certainly the best choice for an interesting experience.

The ground was covered with a few inches of snow but it was a clear, sunny day. For this lesson, I had brought in the rest of the horses, prepared Phantom and told her what our intentions were. When it was time for the girl to lead out, I reminded her to visualize in advance, where she was going to go, and that was to the middle of the field. Once there, I asked the girl to stroke Phantom's neck and to say it was okay. That key is important for our horses. The same would apply before a hoof trim. With it, all went well. For those who found it silly and chose to ignore it, it did not go well at all. I asked the girl to walk with Phantom on a large circle and, eventually, slowly take a distance of a few paces from Phantom. When a circle was completed and a path traced in the snow, I asked Phantom to stand still and we backed off to the full distance of the lunge line. I explained to the girl what her relative position should be as the point of a 'V' between herself with the lunge line to the head of the horse and the lunge whip to the rear. In Quebec, especially where we were located, the language is predominantly French, so the girl would either have to say 'walk' in English or make one clicking sound with her mouth. Trot was also the word, or two click sounds, and canter was the word or four or more click sounds in rapid succession.

I had to teach the horses these universal signals after I first came across that language problem one day on a trail. I was out with someone who had received a gift certificate for either a lesson or a ride. This person had told me she was well experienced with horses and riding. We were separated by some distance after crossing a dangerous section on foot. The rider mounted and said, 'au pas', (pronounced 'Oh pah') which commonly means 'walk' around here. The horse was not responding. Instead of words, a slight forward seat, forward reins, a slight squeeze with the lower leg, one or any combination of those also would have worked. When I turned around to see what was happening, I saw a constant pulling on the reins. The horse most likely would have advanced by himself, but the word, or her intention and the action were completely opposite. The only thing the horse understood from her was her constant pull, so he started to back up. Of course, tension and frustration in both the horse and rider quickly escalated in a matter of seconds and the rider leaned forward to make a whipping movement with the reins, shouted the same vocal cue the she had been repeating and kicked the horse's sides. It would seem that shrill screaming in fear as a horse unexpectedly takes off is also universal. She managed to stay on the horse and I got them to stop when they reached me. It turned out that her experience with horses was a weekend spent with a friend of the family who kept a horse in the back yard and she had taken one riding class at a pony club ten years earlier. The horses were accustomed to the small area that we covered, and I led the way as we first rode out together, so, apparently, she just sat on the horse as he followed me. I discontinued gift certificates.

Back to the story. Phantom understood what was happening and when the girl asked her to walk; she calmly walked with slack in the line. I stayed with the girl and helped her maintain her relevant position. After one turn, I asked her to pick it up to a trot. Phantom made a nice transition and the shy girl managed to say, 'good girl', in English, without any prompt from me. They were doing just fine. After two rounds of trot, I asked her to give the signal for canter and momentarily to gently raise the tip of the lunge whip from the ground. Phantom also did that without blinking an eye. In a way, I was surprised how well the girl and Phantom were doing. The beauty with Phantom is that when she would do anything that we asked it was because, first, she understood, and second, she was willing. When she was with us, she was really with us.

I have seen horses who will comply to demands, and if there is any sign of the horse being reluctant, not doing exactly what the person had in mind, or commonly known as disobedient, then correction or force is used. Eventually, the horse would just explode. For Phantom, if it was an off day or she did not like the person, she would reluctantly comply, but would also make it clear that she was not interested. She would keep asking to be released. She never hurt anyone but her actions were misunderstood and she simply scared the hell out of people. She could make a big fuss and demonstration by shaking her head from side to side, rear, and dart back and forth but without hitting the end of the line. If a person did not take time to reach her in a different way, and force was to be presented, it would be game over. There would not be a chance that anything would be achieved in that session.

After just one round of canter, we stopped there and called to Phantom to come to us. Phantom calmly came to us and stood near the girl as she stroked her. Phantom lowered her head down to the girl and was in one of those rare states where she was very relaxed. It was obvious in her body but you could see it mostly in her eyes. They were big and round, clear and deep and wanting to be there. The girl was completely in rapture and appreciation. Phantom needs that, too. Within minutes, these two had connected so deeply, and it was not because of lunging.

By that time, regular classes, even with a few choice students, were already winding down. The horses would do what was expected of them, but I started to notice that they were not completely happy. Toward the end of a class, it started to show more often that they had enough. During the previous summer, we had set up a course in the field. A narrow pathway to navigate through with turns of ninety degrees. The sides about four inches or ten centimetres high. In order to navigate the horse through a turn, the students had to learn how to control independently the front end and the rear end of the horse. There was also a line of posts that the horse would snake through, like slalom. This was followed by a short tunnel covered in vines, and long troughs filled with flowers as obstacles about one foot or thirty centimetres high. There were also plastic rings suspended from attachments to posts of a temporary dressage ring. The rider would have to get the horse to go along the outside of the fence line with reins in one hand and a plastic sword in the other. They would slowly have to get the horse to close the gap toward the fence in order to snatch up the rings by thrusting the sword through the center of the rings as they galloped along in a steady rhythm.

I explained to the girl the route through which she was to ride Phantom. It was all but the snatching of the rings. They would be walking through the twisting pathway, trotting over one trough, walking a serpentine in between the posts, trotting through the tunnel and going into a canter over another trough. I asked her to explain it back to me, to visualize her and Phantom at the same time, and to point out the course to me as she explained it. Phantom watched her as she did that and looked to the places to which she was pointing. I think that she understood what was about to happen. This whole process may seem ridiculous to some people, but maybe only because I am describing it in detail. Horses already notice a lot more in us than we may perceive.

They are always watching us trying to figure out what we are up to and what they are about to get into. From my perspective, I would be doing this with the horse, and for what I obviously intend, I would not be able to do it without the horse, so I take time to explain what we are going to do together. It always works just fine.

There was one time that a small group of riders stopped at my place. They came from a neighbouring boarding stable. They had seen the course and asked if they could try it. I let them in and a girl of about fifteen years old was just so excited about running the course. I was pleasantly surprised to see the girl take the horse through the course on foot. She wanted to familiarize the horse first. That girl was very excited about it. It was something that she wanted to do. They came from a standard stable, the horses were shod, and they used bitted bridles and old western saddles that weighed a ton. The problem was that as the girl ran along with horse in tow, she was smiling and thrilled as she made her way through the course, but did not notice her horse jerking his head back and his eyes popping out as she was pulling the reins attached to the bit. On one hand, I saw her good intentions, but then the horse seemed to be just an accessory to what she wanted to do. He was not an integral part of the experience. It was not shared. Do you see the difference in that example?

I gave my student a leg up to Phantom and off they went. It was relaxed, well timed, and flawless. They arrived back to me after doing the circuit, I asked the girl to dismount and that was it for the riding that day. I was happy for Phantom, and proud of the girl. That riding was less than three minutes, yet, was a tremendous achievement for the girl. It would be one of the most memorable moments throughout her life. She could accomplish with Phantom that which the majority of my adult students would not even get close. There were very few that I would suggest to partner up with Phantom for a class. I could count them on less than one hand. They had well learned the physical, technical aspect of riding, but there was something essential missing that they could not grasp and was essential with Phantom. It was more the common problem of what they could not get rid of. That, of course, is the ever-present dominant, boss mentality. It is the need for being fully in control at every single moment and afraid of having to adjust to any individual thought or action of the horse. Just like with that smiling, fifteen year old girl pulling her horse around, the horse was a vehicle. It was simply a joy from riding a horse, and it would be the same joy if it were replaced with another horse. The intimate connection to the horse did not truly exist and yet, that connection is what most people seem to be searching. They are in the habit of what they have lived and learned about horses, and when it comes to horses, there seems to be a belief that everything needs to be imposed or trained. They fail to reach out and see what is right in front of them.

My student found Phantom impressive, beautiful, smart, and maybe, just as lonely or misunderstood as she was. I often had students that the only time that I would see them smile was when they were with a horse. It was not simply because they were riding a horse, but because they had a longing to be accepted by the horse and a deep appreciation for whatever the horse would allow, riding or not. The typical view of the Arabian that most people considered violent and dangerous and advised us to put down was actually purposefully delicate and responsive for a twelve-year-old girl riding upon her back. It is not easy to describe and even more difficult to explain how to do it. The main ingredient has to come from the student. In that sense, I did not teach them anything. I presented an opportunity to allow it to flourish. They were opportunities to let that invisible wall finally fall.

Perception

Regardless of what the well-known phrase states, we all tend to judge a book by its cover. We do come to conclusions based on first impressions and we do size up a situation quickly. While this can be useful to us, we can often distort what is in front of us depending on previous experience or expectations.

When I was a kid and after the military experience, I always kept my hair long. However, I lost most of my hair on the top of my head by the time I was thirty. It is incredible how a difference in hair length, style or a variance in colour can change the overall image of a person. Despite my own hair loss, I let my remaining hair to continue to grow. I am the bald guy with long, curly hair. My remaining precious locks are mostly in the back and I usually tie it up in a ponytail. It is not a social or rebellious statement. Perhaps, I am a little too old for that. I just like it, and after all, it is all I have left.

If I am dressed casual and clean-shaven, some people would still think that I am at least a good partyer. If I wear a leather jacket, I could be part of a biker gang or some kind of outlaw. If anyone would see me after an afternoon of playing with the horses, or doing hoof trims, I would often be wearing old, maybe torn clothing, stained with dirt and grass and sweat. People think that I am homeless and hustle their children along to avoid me. If I am dressed in a suit with my hair slicked back, I am a mobster or an assassin. It would be nice if people saw me as a movie star or musician, but I am quiet and reserved and have been told that when I do not smile, I look intimidating. When I used to work in areas that had security posted, and I showed up in a suit and tie, guards would call me sir and let me pass without hesitation. If I went in at an off time, like on the weekend or at night, when I was dishevelled and unshaven and in jeans, the same guards, who happened to be on a rotating shift, actually stopped me for questioning until they realized that they knew me. They never looked at me the same way they did before. The negative image stuck.

The same type of judgment happens toward horses all the time. As boarders, it was blatant and consistent regarding Phantom, but others have also told me of receiving the same type of attitude. It was a snap judgment that someone would make by looking in on someone working in an arena with a horse. All it took was fifteen seconds of someone looking through a window when something unexpected happened and rumours would start either about how bad the horse was or how bad the rider or trainer was or both. I have seen people and horses at stables become labelled and stigmatized. It is sad to say, but most people latch onto such disparagement rather quickly. To some it serves as a form of entertainment. The results could be very hurtful and devastating to both people and horses. Sides have been taken, arguments have erupted, and a mood in a stable could turn so sour that threats are made, fights erupt and people would either get kicked out or decide to move to another stable.

It was rare to find people who shared similar beliefs to be all at one stable. A place where there was cooperation, respect for others' values or equipment or horses, happily shared time for available resources or space. I never saw it during my time as a boarder, but over the ensuing years, did visit private stables where such respect was the norm. What I mean by a private stable is that the doors are not open to just anyone and everyone. The owner will only accept boarders who share the same particular ideals. There were more and more small pockets popping up everywhere. When we were first boarders, the only existing major difference was whether one was riding English or Western. The next differentiation that began to creep in slowly was keeping the horse barefoot. After that, but with less momentum, was riding bitless. The places I was called to were considered alternative. They have moved beyond traditional training and horse keeping. They live more along the lines of the barefoot movement for horses and all it entails, and prefer preventive, natural care or treatments in lieu of standard veterinary practices. They are concerned about saddle fit and although it may still be rare enough, many prefer to ride bitless. With all the advancements and knowledge that has been gathered about the horse, it is almost unbelievable that so few places exist. We may be considered very slow to adapt to such progress in our little part of the world, but at least, I have seen, and thankfully contributed to, such stables being more common and not so strange anymore.

Just like, at a regular stable where some people would not rely on the opinions of others, but of their own first hand thoughtfulness regarding a person or a horse, there are many horse owners with an open mind out there. It is what I call the phenomenon that I see spreading. People who see problems or are uncomfortable with any particular method seek answers. They continually educate themselves, become more independent for themselves and their horses. I consider them driven, intelligent, bold and pioneering. They may not be extroverts or activists, but they pursue a noble cause that is off the beaten path. It takes courage to take action to stand up for your horse. I have frequently been told by different people how they watched in horror, as a trainer would do something to their horse that they would never do themselves. Yet, they remained silent thinking that maybe the trainer knew best, or that they, themselves, did not know better. Those who told me such stories regretted their non-action. However, the experience made them, henceforth, stronger.

Alas, we are human. We have off days, too. I write about the importance of being in the moment, but we often take things for granted. We tend to see things the way that we are thinking about them. A simple example could be to misread a word on a page. This book had to be proof-read by someone else. I could review a page ten times and always miss an error because in my head I knew what the sentence should be and subsequently saw it that way. The error right in front of me was consistently missed. We could often misread a situation or a reaction if we are pressed for time or in urgency. In the book, <u>Blink,</u> by Malcolm Gladwell,[1] he explains the inner workings of our brain and reactions based on our experience and external stimuli. These instant reactions, or suppositions, can sometimes make us see something that is not actually there. I heard that it had become required reading at Columbia Law School and in some police training. I found it to be extremely interesting and informative and can be useful for any type of occupation and daily life.

A local veterinarian unknowingly forever changed my view of how I viewed horses. At that time, I was at a very large stable where I would train horses for the owner who imported them from Shamrock, Saskatchewan. My Big Leo came from the same place. Peppy, the sympathetic horse, the last stallion I was training when that stable was sold, was also from there and ended up as part of our family. That is a different story. In this stable, there was one stallion in regular board. I was warned that this horse had killed two people and that he was unpredictable. Whether true or not, because he was a stallion, people already walked on eggshells around him. Stallions are often treated differently, feared and practically ostracized in a regular stable life. Usually, only one person will handle him and is often left alone and probably put outside less than the other horses. Much less. It was not permitted to put him out of his box and put on crossties in the alley to have his box done. Only the owner of the horse would do it, and it was not done every day. A horse stuck in a box most of the time while seeing others going in and out regularly does not a happy horse make. When the horse becomes so frustrated it only serves to solidify the already inherent fear in people.

The vet came to check the horse's teeth and to float them. He asked me to assist him, and I told him what others had said about the horse being dangerous. As he was slipping into coveralls, he calmly turned his head side to side and said that the horse could be as good or as bad as any other could.

The vet had a sense of calm about him and asked me to keep my own movements gentle and fluid. The horse was a little antsy when we opened the door and, of course, he approached that opening in hopes of going out. I asked the horse to step back with a hand on his chest and I stroked his neck. I was glad that he was not expressive as most horses would be in trying to get a message across. That would be with his mouth by biting. Biting to say, 'Leave me alone', biting to say, 'I'm hungry', biting to say, 'Let me out'. I do not recall exactly how old he was, but he was not an inexperienced youngster and was over four year old. I put the halter on him and attached the lead, and he was calm. I was stroking the base of his neck and the vet said that I should make light, circular motions and to let love flow through my hand. This was a little odd to my ears, especially coming from a vet. I just did not expect that. It did help me to realize that the action alone could be very superficial if done in nervousness or robotic or habitual with little meaning. I did as he asked and I felt the difference. The vet did his work in a slow, deliberate manner and the horse got very relaxed. When we were done and stepped out of the box, he said, 'See? There's nothing wrong with that horse'.

That vet was like a rock that obliterated a crystal sphere of doubt, apprehension and fear that others had formed for me about that horse. Anything could have happened in that box, the horse could have had some serious people issues, but I did learn not to take anything for granted or be prejudiced one way or the other. From then on, that horse looked forward to seeing me because he was very happy when I did come around. I gave him attention and brushed him if no one was around and always acknowledged him if I was just passing by. Although I was not responsible for him, I would clean his box in secret when I had the chance, with him in it. I was the only friend that he had there. I was a little different in my approach with horses, and everyone knew me as the freak who rode bitless, so in a way, he was my only friend there, too.

A similar example about instantaneous false perceptions occurred with Big Leo. One summer, Big Leo developed a sole bruise. The horses are out almost all the time. The only times I usually put them in the barn for a short time is during the winter when there are extreme weather conditions. This would be either a storm fuelled by arctic winds and/or a serious deep freeze, or hail and high winds in the summer. It is almost like having to choose the lesser of two evils. As previously mentioned, we have a good couple of months of wet terrain as winter subsides. That, coupled with walking on snow for at least five months, does open the possibility in spring that a hoof can be damaged with the freedom and exuberance on a warm, sunny day on a section of newly exposed gravel.

I was going to treat the bruised sole in a bucket of water and Epsom salt. Now, as you well know, Leo has done so much with me, and placing his hoof in a bucket of water, to me, was no great task. I was worried about him and could not stand to see him suffer. When I placed his hoof into the bucket, he was reluctant and kept pulling his leg out of the bucket. I got his hoof back in the bucket a couple of times, asked him to stand still, but then he knocked it over as he briskly moved away. This really upset me. He seemed scared and unsure of what we were doing. It got me angry. Here I was trying to help him, and for something as simple as just standing still, which should have been easy for him because of his difficulty walking, he was resisting. He knows my tones of voice and what they mean, very well. I had learned to watch my language, because certain words definitely made him aware of how frustrated I could really be. When he knocked over the bucket and spilled the source of healing, I just turned away and bit my lip in utter disappointment and anger. I did not understand why he would do something like that when I was so concerned about his welfare and trying to make him better. I did not have all day to do this. It took a lot for me to subdue my frustration and just grab the bucket and walk back to the house to refill it. I know full well now, that whether I bide my tongue or not, Leo knows how I feel. That is what helps me now to see, listen, and not instantly react according to my own feelings. What horses do is for a reason.

When I came back with the new mixture, Leo was standing on a soft pile of straw that accumulated over the winter. He was waiting for me and did not move as I approached with the new bucket, and did not resist at all when I placed his hoof in it. It was then that I realized that he was not being uncooperative or fearful by initially removing his hoof and then moving away. He was trying to tell me from the beginning, that he knew I meant well, he was willing to cooperate or, at least, simply listen to me, but he wanted to go to softer ground. Because, when I first did this, to my convenience, it was on the higher, drier, hard area. The area that he got hurt in the first place and was more difficult for him to stand on due to the bruised sole. In other words, he was saying softly, and then loudly, 'Okay, I can do this, but let's do it over there, not here'. I failed to see that. I came to my own conclusions without allowing time for him to show me. Looking back on his reaction, there was nothing different about it, except how I interpreted it.

These are just another couple of examples of why we really need to know our horses well enough, to be open, and to try to comprehend what is going on in the moment. There were multitudes of these little experiences that had led me to a turning point in my life with horses. After all that time and success with training them, I found myself back at where I started. The horses stood before me and after learning so much I was not sure what to do with them anymore. Respect is a big word in the horse world, mostly meaning that horses should just listen to us. Respond, perform, and cause no harm like a well-programmed robot. However, I saw them in a new light now. I had a newfound understanding and respect *for them*.

When the owner of the previously mentioned large stable sold the place, there was still one horse left that I was responsible for selling. I had Peppy for about ten months and he was just over two years old now. The new owner of the facility did not want any kind of business partnership regarding training horses and would charge us the new increased boarding fee. We had to move. We were lucky to find a barn rented out by a farmer to a woman who wanted to start a small, private riding school. It was an old place and I initially felt that it was quite a step down from the modern facilities from which we had moved. For a very reasonable monthly boarding fee, we moved our three horses, plus Peppy, to that old farm.

I had to finish his training and try to sell him. I had arranged that in exchange for free board for Peppy, I would share taking care of all the horses in the place and the cleaning of the boxes. There was only one other boarder there aside from the woman's four horses. I later learned that they shared the rental of the place from the farmer.

Space was tight and there was no indoor manege, but there was a large, outdoor sand ring. I quickly discovered that I enjoyed the privacy compared to the other places we had been. Our horses would go out as a group and we did the most playing at liberty than ever before. As they ran the length of the enclosure in a group, I would guide their direction when they came back toward me. They got used to this and as they would file into the ring for the first time, they fell into single file, began to walk a large circle around me, and waited for the signal to have free reign of the entire space. Seeing them run together with this newfound freedom was thrilling for me. I found the horses seemed more alive and happier. Something changed in their overall look, aside from getting into much better shape.

Everything had been so controlled and subdued at other places. I previously would not have been permitted to play with horses at liberty, especially several at a time, as it was considered too dangerous. In addition, time and access to riding rings were limited. People were too nervous to ride at the same time as I since my horse was without a bit and I sometimes would ride with the other horses loose. With so many boarders, classes or practice going on, it did not allow me to work with young horses or let them loose. People were too afraid. They were not used to seeing untrained horses.

When I used to take the energy-charged Peppy out of his box when people were in the place, they, literally, would clear the alleys. Everyone would run and hide somewhere! The horses and I used to have to make the best of it before 8 A.M. when no one was around.

We had newfound freedom in that old barn. I worked more with Peppy. He knew the basic commands, could be lunged easily, accepted all the tack, and could be handled for grooming, hoof cleaning and stood well on crossties. He came when called and there was no problem for haltering. I knew that the average market was not going to make selling him easy. He was still too young and had no riding experience. To my surprise, someone was very interested in him and finally decided to come down to have a look at him. I was certain that this person was going to buy Peppy. He telephoned me a week after our correspondence and told me he was already on his way. He was travelling over three hours and bringing a horse trailer with him. We were to meet at the barn, but that day the woman was there in the morning to take care of chores. I advised her of the meeting and told her I would be there soon. She had put the horses outside and the buyer got there before I did.

As I was driving there, the reality of selling Peppy began to sink in. I was thinking that I had trained and sold other horses without having an emotional attachment to them as strong as it was with Peppy. The thought of Peppy going away brought tears to my eyes. It made me very sad, but I knew that I could not keep him.

When I arrived, they were standing at the fence of the

outdoor ring. The buyer was just watching Peppy move around and immediately wanted to negotiate a much lower purchase price. Peppy came from a reputable breeder and was a registered Paint Horse. He did not come cheap even as a colt. The guy talked as if he would be doing me a favour by taking him off my hands. He told me that he would be willing to settle for Peppy because his plan was to have fun doing barrel races during the approaching summer. He would then sell him for meat in the autumn to get some money back. I thought I was hearing things. There was to be no deal when I heard those words and I even increased my price to assure that. No price would make me change my mind. As soon as the guy left, I called the owner of the former stable and told him I was going to buy Peppy from him. I was not quite sure how I could afford it, but I had grown attached to Peppy.

I brought Peppy back inside the barn and the woman asked me if the sheet attached to his door was really for him. All the things that Peppy could do were written on that sheet. I found it extensive and was quite proud of it. She found it amusing because once she released Peppy outside, she was not able to get him back when the guy arrived. He did not come when called and she barely got the halter back on him. That situation rubbed her ego the wrong way. This was the first sign regarding the type of relationship I was forming with the horses, but, at that time, all her statement did was leave me perplexed. Peppy did do all those things with me; I could not understand why he did not do it that day. Unfortunately, my assumption that he would behave the same way with anyone was not altered in any other way. It just seemed odd to me, and then I forgot about it, because I had no problem handling Peppy.

The woman renting the old barn wanted to give classes but that did not bode well with the rental partner who was the one other boarder. Due to the conflict between them, she took her horses and left. Now there were only our four horses and that one boarder. I was lucky to work out the same type of boarding arrangement with him regarding Peppy. He lived and worked nearby, so he would feed the horses at the start of the day. I would be there as of mid-afternoon until late evening. His horse was really for his daughter and she was in school, so the horses and I pretty much had the place to ourselves. I managed to work out an arrangement to pay for Peppy, too. We had a new member of the family, relative freedom and privacy.

The Day it all Changed

Was there one specific moment that forever changed my way with horses? I can say that there indeed was a huge catalyst. The big event in my life with horses happened in the summer of 2005. I had a 5 year old Haflinger and owner to train for trail rides. Both were inexperienced. With previously not riding Leo for so long, I had learned how to do a lot of groundwork and developed a knack for anticipating a horse's reaction. I found that groundwork was much more important than our pressing goal to get on a horse. To me, judging how they felt seemed obvious by just looking at the horse. I was lucky to start this without putting my own emotions into any type of interpretation. That is so easy to fall into but just on the surface, their reactions are not unlike ours. This could include puzzlement in the eyes, apprehension in the brow, and tenseness in the muscles. My main goal was to have the horse learn and stay relaxed, and that simple differentiation was easy to spot, so force and physical violence were not used. That also excludes what most people consider not violent. A bit, to me, is violent. Research has proof of the detrimental effects of the bit. It has even been presented to the FEI, but although a relatively recent controversial training method called rolkur, or hyper-flexion was ruled against after presentations by veterinarians regarding the dangers of that, they could not do the same regarding the bit. According to Dr. Cook, who at the time of the writing of this book, was the last person to rally for the abolition of the bit, or to at least, optionally allowing Bitless Bridles into competition, stated that their reasons to ignore scientific study were for adherence to tradition. The FEI`s code regarding the welfare of the horse was put to the wayside in this instance due to overwhelming adherence to habit. I also did not hit the horse in any way for correction. What about using a chain over the nose for correction or immobilization? Out of the question. Same as chasing the horse with a whip. No shaking lead lines attached to the horses' head, or prodding with sticks. No slapping. Reassurance was one of my main tools, and with patience, I would find ways to help the horse understand what I wanted. It always worked.

Part of the illumination I experienced that summer was again related to the feelings or actions of the horse. Horses that I worked with at home would be so good with me. They would also be pretty good with the owner if I were present. If an owner showed up when I was not around, I would hear that they could sometimes not even halter the horse and would completely give up and leave in anger and frustration. Why did this seem familiar to me? Specifically, with that horse and owner, after such an incident, I later demonstrated how I went about things with the horse. The horse would come to me when called, be easily haltered, lead into a field of grass and stand still while I backed off and walked a large circle around him. The owner's jaw dropped and said that he seemed like a completely different horse. This made me ask myself some questions: What was happening? What was I not doing right in teaching the people? Why could they not do what I did, even if I gave them classes once, twice, or three times per week? What I realized, was that my horses, or all the horses I trained, because no force and pain were involved, were not `broken`. It was a trust and a bond that we developed. This trust and bond, comprehension, and willingness were part of our unique relationship. That relationship was not transferable.

Since the horse was boarded at our home, when the owner would visit just to spend an afternoon with the horse, they had, perhaps, the misfortune of me hovering about. I would be like a voice on her shoulder just making comments. `Do this`, `don't do that`, `Watch for this`, `Give him a second`, `don't pull`, etc. Things improved. It had a lot more to do with a person's attitude, confidence and certainty than the horse. More importantly, time spent with the horse. Then came mutual understanding and cooperation and they started to be able to have fun together. I was very proud of the efforts and success that both students had obtained.

The main objective for the owner was to be able to ride that horse in trail. Some classes were short rides on trails with which the horse was already familiar. That trail was across the main road. It is used mostly as a skidoo trail in the winter. In the summer, it is a variety of sections of full surface rock, gravel, sand, dirt. Open spaces of wild bush and tall grass on either side of that rough road that gently winds up and down and eventually leads into the forest. The main road that I mention is significant because it cuts through this forest and the inhabitants here have clear patches of land etched alongside each side of it. We are located in the lower quarter of this forest, which is immense. It stretches north as far as the eye can see. It is very sparsely populated to non-populated areas.

The horse was doing fine and we agreed it was time to ride out to explore a new area together as a practice. This would be on my side of the road. It started out with a section of pine trees that made an open, canopied space to walk through and rose to a plateau of tall grass and shrubs. I always liked the calmness in there. Diffused light, coolness from the summer heat and a layer of pine needles carpeting the forest floor. From there, it was a clear, open area with very rocky terrain. In our area, almost any area is rocky, but this more than most. Then flat fields that stretched out to civilization. It is only 24 acres and belongs to a farmer that gave me permission to go there with horses. It was a beautiful day. I had seen a doe and two of her young grazing in the field beside us just that morning. We both looked forward to the outing with confidence and anticipation.

We saddled up the horses and led them out. We walked alongside the road that runs across the façade of the field where the deer were earlier. Regardless of my faith in the steadfastness of the horses, I never ride along that road. I certainly do not have faith in the people who speed down it. When we were in the forest, we mounted and I heard, what I assumed were, the deer running in the forest, off to the side of us. I was not worried. The horses had seen deer before on a daily basis. They had even stood face to face across the fence to that field.

It is understood that we rode only using the Bitless Bridle and the horses barefoot. I know the bit would not stop the horse and yet still used only the BB as very light signals. This was already due to a lot of groundwork or practice. We made our way and the horses navigated well on some rough terrain. When we entered the fields that lead to the houses at the end, we decided to head back. There was a small work shack with men cutting logs and they did not seem to like our presence on the private land. We dismounted at some points along the way back to take pictures with the horses. The adventure was over and we were getting close to the pine forest again.

On the narrow trail, not much wider than the width of a horse, with grass and bushes growing 3-5 feet high on either side, a deer ran straight across it. That was straight across the path of the owner and the horse ahead of me. I saw the deer's head come out of the grass, heard half a scream, and when I blinked, I was turned about 180 degrees at full gallop. Her horse had spun. He flew past my horse and me in the opposite direction in which we were headed. In the spin, he lost the rider. My horse reacted and followed. It was like changing channels on a television. One moment it was a calm, peaceful stroll across the countryside, and then it was full horsepower, dust flying under thundering hooves in a panic run for life. I regained my senses, was asking my horse to stop (with reins) while calling out to the horse ahead to `whoa`. He did. I was actually surprised. As I dismounted, I thought of possible bad reactions from loggers at a small shack that were just beyond the location where we had turned back. I kept eye contact with the horse, felt the necessity of him having to come back. By the time I was standing on the ground, he was already coming back. Outwardly, he appeared perfectly calm. He and my horse stood together while I went to pick up the owner who hit the rocks like wet newspaper. We managed to ride out together. The horses continued with us as if nothing had happened. However, a lot happened.

I fully realized that it is not any kind of our means of control that makes a good horse. Yet, I understood that a long time before. My tag line for the business was, 'No such thing as a bad horse'. Was I still not teaching the horse to accept some form of means of control? I automatically believed that a means of physical control was absolutely necessary. Rather, I just never thought that maybe it was not. It was not much different from when I first believed that a bit was necessary. The equipment that I used was slightly different, but I did not change how it was used at all. This was the day I realized that it was not what is on the horse's head that counts, but what is inside it. Plus, and more importantly, the understanding and the trust the horses have in us because we take the time to help them understand, and not just make them react to a physical, topical, or restraining pressure. This, as well, was nothing new to me. In writing this book, I highlight some of the horses that showed that to me. I saw a little here, and grasped a little more there, but it never all coalesced as it did on this particular day. In a matter of seconds, I finally broke away from that linear way of thinking. What I believed as the best physical means to control the horse, through the Bitless Bridle, however softer than most, was blown away that day. Though the Haflinger was in fear and panic, he listened to me and stopped when I called to him. The potential of what a horse is capable of finally became known. That horse was about a hundred feet, or thirty metres, ahead of me, without a rider, and when I told him it was okay, he believed me and came back. It was a connection stronger than any rope or bridle.

Yet, I was traumatized at all this. My immediate, main concerns were the injuries of my student - physical and emotional. However, if she had not fallen, I wonder if the ensuing events would have been the same? How much longer would it have taken all my little ideals to come together to create a brand new outlook? I had been moving further on up the track, but the track was exactly the same. Yet, like in the past, the horses showed me something that day that reverberated in my soul. I could not have sat down that day and wrote these realizations. I felt it, but could not really intellectualize and express it. I was still too analytical about what I thought I had learned about horses. It was an accumulation of many small experiences, with different horses, that kept hinting at something more. Even in my way of doing things with horses, I had not seen the simplicity that they so often presented before me. Yet, simply calling to the young horse and his response brought all my subconscious thoughts and experiences together. Maybe I was in denial because it would have a huge impact on my career. I felt lost and dazed because this event finally had just turned my seemingly perfect world with horses upside down. I wished that all those horses from my past that had given me those hints could see me now.

This is one of those topics that are difficult for me to describe. On the surface, most people would not find anything extraordinary about that event. All is well that ends well. Simply get back in the saddle and continue on. As with riding without a bit, most people would say that it is possible on a particular horse because that horse is a good horse or has the quiet temperament for it. Such a comment only justifies how many `good` horses there are out there.

Only in retrospect do I see how much faith the rider had in the horse to be able to get back in the saddle after such a fall. If she was apprehensive, it did not show. I would have understood if she wanted to walk out on foot. It is a common story coming from riding schools or trail rides that when someone falls off a horse, that it is imperative that they get right back on. This is insisted upon regardless of the state of the horse or the fear in the person. That, too, can help one appreciate how a horse sometimes feels. To feel like we have no choice; forced despite our fears; forced despite protestations; our feelings or thoughts not respected. It is demoralizing and it hurts. We must be realistic, too. That young horse, with little experience, out of his habitual and safe environment was suddenly surprised. Which came first? Did the horse spin because of the surprise of the deer and his reaction made the woman scream? Did the woman scream because of the surprise of the deer, which then resulted in the horse to choose to run?

What some may say could have avoided the initial reaction to the deer suddenly crossing the trail or the scream would be to recondition the reaction in the horse. Completely alter his natural instinct, his own safety mechanism. Train the horse to freeze instead of going into flight when a frightening stimulus is presented. That idea sounds nice to suit our needs; however, what do you think the horse will have to go through to get close to that reaction? Not only would I find that to be abnormal, but even I, as a supposedly superior human, know that my wife is in the house, and if she came up quietly behind me and put her hand on my shoulder while I was writing this, I would probably still jump a foot off the chair. This was not about training anymore.

Although not instant, changes ensued because of the results of that day. I stopped giving riding lessons to the public at a large stable. I maintained only a handful of those existing students for private classes at my place with my own horses. When the package of lessons was over, I did not permit renewals. In rare cases, I would still accept a horse for training at my home, because that is what I enjoyed most. However, I found that by doing so, I was still hanging on to a career, a service to the public that I did not believe in anymore. It was a matter of a few months before I closed the doors of my established business for good.

The Crossroads

Waseskun is a Cree word meaning the dispersion of clouds after a storm and the moment when the sun breaks through with blue skies. Standing outside at night, feeling and smelling the air, the noises of nature and the sky speckled with starlight, the ground aglow from a shining moon is also like opening a door for my spirit. I would have the same feeling in a quiet sunrise. Life does not change much around us, but our perception of it does. Sometimes it could change drastically from one day to the next.

While looking over some old notes it is interesting to see what I wrote, what I thought, how I felt years ago, or even not so long ago. Sometimes it seems that it is just such a world away, not even coming from me. It can be a rediscovery of ourselves. To see where we have been still helps in knowing more of where we have arrived.

We all need to be heard and to be understood by those around us. Yet, is that not the ego? Somehow, sometimes, what can be perceived as a hindrance permits us indirectly to unveil a better part of ourselves. However, it is all too common that we usually first stumble along the way and make big mistakes.

Some of my best thoughts that were put into words were due to an inner frustration caused by unthinking words shot onto the wind by others. At least I have the peace within myself to come back with my own perspective and it has usually been successful in being able to share. Instead of a counter-attack, it deflates and completely shifts the dialogue, feeling, and thought. A shift, which I believe, circumvents the ego and permits honest evaluation. A shift toward compassion, understanding and beauty to which I believe the human heart is very susceptible.

I still wonder if I have any real understanding. For my interpretations are only what my human mind can comprehend about our world. What I have mostly discovered about myself, and by which I try to live, is not the standard with which we have all been raised. It is not left-brain thinking as we learned in school and utilize in all the overall challenges we face in daily life.

The two halves of the brain are distinct and connected to each other only through a cable of nerves called the corpus collosum. Mention of this has nothing to do with existing interpretations about the horse perception and certainly not about interpretation about horse personalities.

The 1981 Nobel Prize Winner, Roger Sperry,[1] in his studies to understand more of how each side functioned, worked out a map of how each side interpreted the world. The left side of the brain controls the right eye or right side of the body, while the right side of the brain controls the left side of the body. In studies following the medical procedure to control epileptic seizures, by cutting the link between the two hemispheres, or corpus collosum, the understanding of each side of the brain became clearer. They both functioned but could not share information that is often crucial in our daily existence. For example, the logical part of the brain, the left, when shown a picture of a horse, could read or write the word 'horse', but could not describe what a horse is. The right side could explain what a horse is used for or what it does, but could not name it. That is, if the image was perceived at all. The right side understands and produces images, symbols, feelings, in a non-verbal way. Sperry believes that the right side or creative side of the brain is greatly suppressed in the educational system and society. Most children are highly creative, but after entering school, only ten percent remain so by the age of seven. Only two percent retain this type of high creativity as adults.

The full expression of the right brain is subsequently often confined to release only through meditation or dreams. It is the experience of receiving and giving in any given moment, and mostly, the feeling. I can give an example that I think most adults may have experienced. A dream can be vivid, although bizarre, but the imagery and feeling creates perfect understanding. It all makes sense. Upon waking and recalling the dream and trying to analyze the great revelation of it, the left-brain quickly dominates once more and none of it makes sense. It is no longer understood and the real feeling or message, no matter how beautiful the dream may have been and made us feel, becomes only a detached memory. Logic prevails.

This is, perhaps, why I feel that it can be difficult to explain what I personally realized with my experience with horses. Why I seemed to come to decisions or realizations, but could not rationally explain it. Daily life can be made a little easier with this, but I find it most rewarding, profound, or clearer when I am with the horses only. It could be better expressed, visually, through paintings. An exceptional artist would be able to invoke a clear message without words. People viewing it could feel such a clear message, but be unable to put the feeling into words. The same could be understood through what music can convey. Sometimes, we have to learn to allow such feelings to guide us without rational explanation. How that is individually handled could make a big difference to how we are perceived by the rest of society. I cannot fully state that it is easier to hate than to love, but hate seems so much more abundant. There is a lot in the world that I wish I could change. I believe that there was an ancient knowledge that was lost that we are slowly rediscovering again on our own. It seems to be a shadow of a memory within us. It seems to be a growing yearning for a more harmonious existence within the world.

After all the various experiences and enlightenment provided by horses that helped change my own beliefs and fixed ideas which culminated in the experience with the Haflinger, I was lucky enough to discover that I was not alone with such thoughts. Although I knew that what I learned must have previously existed somewhere, there was no available set standard for this. Despite all the equine studies I found through research, those results did not generally affect the way that people used horses. Of course, we know that new training methods appeared, but at the end of the line, horses were expected to do the same things as always.

At this point, I had already reduced my classes to a few choice students who easily understood, and were very happy to work with, my accrued principles. However, these classes were mainly with my own horses and I could see that there were days when the horses really did not want to have to partake in any of that. It was interesting to see when particular students showed up; the horses would either come to the fence or run away to the opposite end of the field. A horse may have been willing at the beginning of the class, but also started to show signs of being fed up toward the end of it. Using Dr. Cook's bitless bridle was fine, but I knew that the horses were still forced at times to maintain a desired path. A less damaging means of control, but an imposed control nonetheless. After, what I consider, horses showing me a side of them that was so personal, I was already trying to find a way out of that standard result of just riding horses. As mentioned before, I did end up closing that side of my business but not before discovering what was to become very controversial in the horse world.

Why was it controversial? Because it did not simply advocate non-violence and respect for horses, it also stood by its scientific findings for the welfare of the horse. It revealed the negative physiological responses in horses affecting overall soundness and neurological and myological (muscle) damaging and cascading effects from standard horse use and training and equipment. It cast aside any of those standard norms of human control over the horse. What that means is to educate a horse without punishment, without any physical restraints, without inducing pain or the fear of it. No force, no bridles, no bits, no spurs, and in keeping with the welfare of the horse, no horseshoes. To most non-horse people that would seem to make perfect sense. To private horse owners, it seemed like a dream come true. To the standard horse world it was, literally, unbelievable.

The NHE Experience

It was through Dr. Cook that I met a collaborative researcher named Lydia Nevzorova. She had written articles for horse magazines in Russia, was an accomplished photographer and used thermography to help illustrate and educate about the damage caused to a horse's back by bad saddle fit and riding. She had created a website highlighting her work and that of her husband, Alexander Nevzorov. He was passionate about the old school Haute Ecole and was determined to find a way to work with a horse that absolutely rejected any kind of equipment. Haute Ecole is rare in the world today. One of the most famous existing schools is the Spanish Riding School of Vienna. Most of the moves performed by the horses are similar to what they do at liberty by instinct during play, mating or fighting. It is a way of working with horses to get them into exceptional shape both physically and mentally.

At the time, Alexander was not very interested in the science side of things. Lydia was the one studying in England to learn more about hippology. He discarded all that he had previously learned about working with horses. As stated by Alexander, it was the horse that interested him: a horse as a sentient, very intellectual, suffering and spiritual being that was so humiliated by humans. He learned to understand that it was not his talent that really mattered but his approach and the feeling that he was no longer hiding from horses. Love and endless respect was the greatest instrument of all.

When this information initially began to become available outside of Russia, fully understanding it and even expressing it proved quite a challenge. It was not an approach that was already set in stone. It was an ongoing revelation of what is possible with horses to what had been learned up to that point. In the West, people are used to being handed complete little packages through marketing that provide a program showing how to start and extolling the benefits that can be obtained by following through right to the end. However, with this new approach, it was not so. It was an often misunderstood philosophy coming out of St-Petersburg. For me, timing was perfect. I had stumbled into what is known as Nevzorov Haute Ecole (NHE).[1] An internet forum, in Russian, already existed and by helping to launch the international forum in English is where I learned the monumental difference between simple translation and subtle interpretation.

I quickly saw through the forum medium that the acceptance of these new ideas and the rapidity of learning were more pronounced by those in Russia. On the English side, many simply could not escape the mindset of the traditional ways or other methods that continued to cling to them. The greater success rate on the Russian side may have been because there was not much available in terms of different training techniques. Even the rules within the Russian Equestrian Federation for competition, or acceptance of how people could treat horses, is appalling. The overall existing method was traditional horse training, which was very harsh, and often way over the top. For example, whipping to the point of drawing blood from the horse, in training or competition, was considered normal. Even in the West, an expression of teaching the horse a lesson behind the barn still exists. In Russia, teaching a horse a lesson for not performing well in competition by getting a group of men together and restraining the horse and whipping with chains is commonly accepted.

The lack of information proliferation from the West about horses and training them available within Russia permitted many people to wish or seek for a better way. They were not analyzing or comparing different techniques, which are so abundant in the West. Their thought was not clouded by different methods, perceptions, or interpretations that may have been instilled earlier. Many, especially the younger generation, were disgusted with the treatment of horses all around them and they embraced NHE.

From my experience with horses and what I understood from Lydia and Alexander, a common phrase within the forum to try to help people begin to grasp what NHE was about was, 'forget everything that you have learned'. So much time and energy was initially spent, not directly helping people progress with NHE, but trying to diffuse the endless barrage of arguments against it. Many people had doubts or even frustration in grasping what we were trying to reveal. Seeing information is one thing, but thinking about it and even going out there and trying to experience it is what really counts. I often repeated myself by writing that `teachers point the way but only you can find the place`. Well, that only means something to someone once it is lived. Nevertheless, everyday, there was at least one person who came to understand or learn some important aspect. Sometimes, they were stunned because it could turn their world upside down. After pondering such an exchange on the forum, or understanding something within this book, in the end, it is usually a horse that will prove it.

The horse has served us throughout history for facilitating survival and for war; there was no time, or much desire, to build a nice relationship. Yet, there have been many examples in history of people who realized and understood that this was possible and lived it. In that regard, NHE is nothing new. However, what may be different is applying the philosophy to schooling to Haute Ecole level. All this without force.

On one hand, it was all so simple. So many people in the world do not know about or follow any particular method geared toward training horses. They live a kind of parallel or semblance to NHE philosophy and have unique relationships with their horses without ever hearing about NHE. On the other hand, a lot of dispute arose perhaps due to what people may consider a good relationship. Many were insulted or deeply hurt because our version of a good relationship included what was good for the horse, not just the human, as previously mentioned in the section, *Communicating Like a Horse*.

There are certainly cultural differences of all societies, but when it comes to the human/horse relationship, it seems people, the world over, share the fundamental quest for truly being able to reach the horse. Yet, on this subject regarding the horse, a recurring problem in the search is... 'Not being able to see the forest because of the trees'.

There were mistakes made in the beginning by still trying to relate to and by referring to existing methods of training. It was not long before we realized that once we were looking beyond hopeful notions, or ways to help people relate to what we were trying to describe, the details of any other existing training method was imposing force or manipulating the horse. That was obviously counter to what we had learned and the philosophy within NHE. However, most people understood that we did not just drop out of the sky with new wisdom. We, too, had followed a similar road with horses and had to overcome many of the same mistakes, beliefs and habits and continue to forge ahead in what we believed.

Lydia's photos of their horses in action with Alexander were so beautiful and astounding that news of NHE quickly spread. What surprised me was not the amount of people who did not believe that this was possible, but those who spent an enormous amount of energy trying to disprove it. Unfortunately, many did not see the wider scope beyond Alexander. He was not trying to promote himself as a trainer or the only one getting results. There were many success stories in Russia, I had also achieved results, and so did my students. As different as NHE is, so are the schools. They are not open to the public - in the sense that someone can pull up and ask to sign up their kids for classes - as is the norm for riding schools, for example. Actually, the real school exists online found through the NHE website. It is more a source of information, sharing of ideas and experiences and networking.

I refused 90% of requests for classes. It is really a way of life with horses. It has nothing to do with training. Holding on to the old mentality that we have been taught all our lives is where the problem lies. Try explaining this new way to someone who has spent not only a large part of their life learning traditional methods, but also thousands of dollars on trainers and riding classes. It is how one views the horse and interacts that makes all the difference in the world. I had many requests for clinics, and again, especially at the beginning, most people expected to have a horse put into an enclosure, and watch results from a few hours of forced groundwork. That is what people are used to. That is not what we do.

I believe that I served as an important buffer between what was coming out of Russia to the rest of the world. Alexander stands steadfastly beside what he has lived and learned about horses. Whether intentional or not, his method of presenting facts was also controversial. To say that many people in the West found him to be arrogant or insulting would be an understatement. I once had a discussion with a publisher who was interested in his book, <u>The Horse Crucified and Risen</u>[2], and they found it too direct, or harsh, and suggested that I rewrite the entire book with him to tone things down. I understood Alexander enough at that time to know that he would never accept compromise. In presenting his findings, he wanted people to think and to rise above blissful ignorance.

People outside of Russia misconstrued him as a new player in the horse-training world who was presenting a new technique. People were expecting training videos but they were getting creative, elaborate documentaries. Was he being elusive? Was he trying to keep secrets? Was he a charlatan? Many people still do not understand how NHE, as it is known today, fully came about.

He was a TV news reporter and talk show host. He continues that main media career through film making. His approach with his horses became a great idea to present to the studio. Two of his several passions could be combined into one. He never intended to be a horse trainer to the public. His approach in media is very direct and he is a professional in knowing how to create a stir. It is great for television ratings in Russia, but taken a little against the grain in the outside world. Yet, to deal with the man on a personal level is very different. He is a focused leader, but also with depth, heart and respect for others.

What he presented about horses was so different, created such praise and uproar from the public after the release of his first made-for-television film that Lydia decided to create a website and forum to handle the enormous reaction and influx of comments and questions. With the creation of the online forum, it began to take on a life of its own because the international public automatically forged it into a new direction as a training medium. Alexander never wanted to go public in that way. Lydia wanted to help people understand the plight of horses by bringing facts to light and encouraging people to open their eyes to what was really around them. As an activist, she created the Horse Revolution to help change rules, laws and standards regarding horses in Russia. That was the initial, main goal of their message.

Alexander slowly became more involved in the growing NHE virtual world and started to present more of his personal views and many people hung on his every word. The problem was that the rich Russian language was sometimes translated to very base English, and often, with erroneous results. Another problem that surfaced occasionally was that many people saw NHE as the new iconic standard for horse keeping. Situations and rules of his school about horse keeping in Russia did not always apply to the outside world, and were sometimes impossible to apply due to existing laws in different countries. Lydia was continuously learning about natural hoof trimming and the barefoot lifestyle for horses. They had not created anything new but I envied the environment they had created for their horses. However, articles or statements released by Alexander covering different topics at once sometimes caused confusion. This was due to his interest in the history of old school methods conflicting with what people assumed was his own advice on the proper keeping of horses. Those who were still waiting to understand or wrongly understood his method were as easily confused by new, general information while forgetting the initial, overall revelation.

What the NHE website and my own published articles presented created a very large appeal. However, during the first year, I do not think there was one geographical area outside of Russia where a like-minded group of people could meet locally to discuss NHE topics or ideals. The location for people to come together was the online forum and it was filled with people from all over the world. To the dismay of many, what made the crucial differentiation of this forum and others is that people were expected to join only if they already supported the ideals. It was not an open forum about various horse-training techniques. We had already made the mistake of mentioning other techniques to simply inform people or as quick fixes to buy a horse time. The people who were to join were expected to have already gone through those phases or experiences and realizations. Because of the intolerance of bending the rules, or how they had an impact on the most common, standard, accepted, universal beliefs about horse use, it did not get very far with the average rider who wanted to recount their weekend trail ride.

Passion about horses ranges far and wide. There were certainly serious detractors regarding NHE, as well as, pockets of very passionate people, that some considered fanatics, supporting it. Interestingly enough, those initial perceptions of roles of others sometimes reversed. At times, those within the virtual network perceived typical human behaviour as catastrophic to the cause. Indeed, it could be. People wanted to belong to something important, different, with strong values and that did not bow to commercialism. If there was a rumour about someone in the NHE team doing something that was anywhere close to going against the welfare of the horse, or philosophy behind NHE, some members could be devastated and completely walk away for feeling that they had been betrayed. Some from the outside who came to secretly investigate what this controversial forum was all about, looked at information and became real forum members or, at least, knew it was not for them, but changed some previously learned aspect to improve the life of their horse.

Aside from the fact that the message from NHE was not fully understood, or often misinterpreted, many people who wanted to be part of it were not completely honest. It would hardly be a surprise to me, but I tried to keep a focus on the bigger picture. I considered Lydia's mission and vision greater than any particular incident or isolated circumstance. That is easy to say, but it was not easy for me and others to personally deal with a lot of people who got emotionally hurt, insulted, or felt rejected. It was not easy to witness such beautiful ideals and accomplishments with horses become surrounded by an atmosphere of personal attacks and rebuttals. It wore people down, including me. However, it is interesting to see that although a large majority of people, who admitted to themselves that they could not make the change from regular horse use or competition, still admired Alexander and Lydia. People who chose not to adhere to the philosophy remained impressed about what they were able to do with horses. It was a constant challenge to maintain that bridge between two worlds or even function within them. What Alexander and Lydia achieved with horses is very real and they continue as strong advocates for the protection of the horse.

Since I bring up NHE here as part of my personal experience, I feel that I should give a further explanation as to what it is about. The following is an article that I wrote for Natural Horse Magazine,[3] Volume 10, Issue 2 in March 2008. It was after most of my main articles explaining NHE had already been published, but I went on to do a question and answer series. This one was from someone who was seeking harmony with her horse and after studying other methods, really wanted to know how to achieve it. The article includes some of what I may have already mentioned in this book, and repeats parts of what I had often wrote about in previous articles or other Q&As. However, I leave the original article in its entirety to give a general perspective of NHE. Besides, expressing the same thought in a slightly different manner helps different people understand it clearly.

***

Harmony

It is wonderful to want to work in harmony and peace with horses. However, what is most difficult for people can depend on what it is we want to do with horses.

If I ask, `Were horses created for riding? `, more than 99% of people say no. However, if we take a look at the horse world around us, not only the real horses, but toys, plush horses complete with bits and reins, depictions in paintings, books, movies and television, the truth is that people actually think, `what else is a horse for?`.

If you have studied other methods, then you well know that what you read in a book, or even hear what some trainers say and then what they actually do with the horse can be quite a contrast.

It is not necessarily a matter of knowing what is right or wrong, good or bad. The horse is no longer a need, or very useful, for survival to humans as in centuries past. Things have changed. However, the horse is still often perceived as a subservient animal that continues to serve for our own entertainment. I do agree that many people simply follow the norm and while learning, take everything as fact. The existing methods certainly work.

I want to point out what I just wrote above about viewing the horse as a subservient animal. NHE gets rid of this. We are on a level playing field. We are two `creatures` that need to learn how to communicate. Right there, that could be a big problem for a lot of people.

Yet, what is also important in NHE is what goes beyond that... or should I say, before? The health of the horse is paramount. Lifestyle and living conditions play a very important role.

I do ride my horses, but it is in a different context than how most people ride today. It is still working toward physical strength of the horse. The motto of the school is, `The Horse is always right`. It may be considered that NHE is a physical fitness program for domesticated horses. It is personal because once building a relationship and understanding and subtle communication between oneself and a horse, that trust, bond, relationship is not transferable. In other words, we cannot `train` a horse with the mentality of NHE and expect the horse to act the same with someone else as they do with us. Those who want to build a relationship should take that relationship as it comes, and not because it is only a step to being able to ride a willing horse. Do you see the difference?

In general terms, this means that if a horse refuses, there is a good reason. What we hear most of the time is that the horse is lazy, stubborn, or stupid. In reality, it is usually, but not always, because of some kind of physical discomfort.

With other methods, the horse can be coerced to continue to perform, but most people do not know the consequences that the horse suffers. It is sad that what is considered normal today, in terms of common horse ailments, can and should be avoided.

At best, with a perfectly sound horse, it can also take very long to get understanding, practice, strength and fluidity within just one movement. A good Spanish Walk could take two years. When I have requests from dressage riders how to do a piaffe, I suggest a good dressage trainer instead. When I get a request of how to make a horse lay down, I suggest trick training. NHE is not a 'method' where someone can pick out just a thing or two. It is a way of life, of thinking, of being. It is the result of what many people, worldwide, have expressed about wanting to be with their horses. I think it is marvellous and I am somewhat surprised at this apparent shift in consciousness or behaviour and the increase of change of thought toward the horse based on the type of requests that I get from around the world. Nevertheless, it is still very difficult for people to change their ways or to break old habits, even when pursuing NHE. Unless, there is a major incident that we experience with a horse or seeing with our own eyes a great tragedy, plus an accumulation of little self-denials, where everything in our brain about what we have learned about horses short-circuit in an instant. In addition, when it comes to harmony or friendship with horses, many people would like to have their cake and eat it too. As you mention, presently, the horse will be okay as long as he sticks with you and your ideas. Otherwise, there can be hell to pay, is there not? A horse that has no choice but to obey may be harmony and peace for what you want, but is it for the horse? This is also an important differentiation in the meaning of the words (harmony, friendship, willingness) that people use.

Many people think that NHE is withholding secrets. I was initially very reluctant to travel to fulfill requests for lessons. I thought the website would be enough. NHE is so simple, why would I have to meet people and their horses in person? However, learning from a page on a computer screen is far removed from our reality of being out in the field with horses, or living the experience, or seeing a live reaction. I think that people have a hard time understanding how simple this really is. Pages and pages of documents cannot replace noticing the look in a horse's eye when that moment of understanding takes place or seeing a side of the horse's character that was never seen before. Let me explain further. Consider that you come across a child in a remote, tropical forest. This child does not speak your language, and notices that you carry a ball. This child has never even seen a ball and does not even know what to do with a ball. How would you get this child to understand that you are not a threat, and how would you show what a ball is for, and even eventually get this child to willingly, happily play with you? Put the child in a cage? Secure with a rope to prevent escape while you prove that the ball is not harmful by bringing this alien object closer? Prod the child with a stick to get closer to the ball? Put chains around the wrists and drag to the ball? Threaten with imminent aggression until the child gets near the ball and then relax and smile? Every step closer to the ball, you give the child a candy? etc, etc...

I am sure you know the list. All of them would work. Putting it this way tends to insult people. What I like about the younger generation is that they see right through all that typical training stuff right away. They immediately question and do not follow. I have never seen that before. Trying to communicate and become understandable is not a method or a type of training. That is why the shift in mentality of how we view the horse is so important. I have seen people want to achieve the results seen within NHE, yet they feel quite foolish while trying to play with the horse or become understandable without using usual training techniques. What they are really seeking is a result and want an immediate response from the horse. In such a situation, the person will become angry, decide that NHE is absolutely ridiculous, and pull out either a whip or a clicker instead. It does not matter what method they fall back on, they go back to training an animal.

Another example question of our communication and understanding by the horse would be how would you show a horse to lift a leg without touching? How would you ask a horse to pick up a halter from the ground? How would you get a horse to pick up the blue halter instead of the red one? Yes, this is all possible. Just try asking the horse!

Health and lifestyle are important. Some would say that their horses just love going out on trail rides. Yes, it is quite possible because the horse has been in a box for a week or all day. Fed like humans (2-3 meals per day) and given sweet feed, another tradition, which is not good for horses. Whenever the horse goes out it is for some human reason. In some cases, they may get out for one hour out of twenty-four. Some people choose to leave the horses outside. Unfortunately, often this is not based on physical or mental welfare reasons for the horse, but a financial one. Even if the horse is outside, are the conditions acceptable? Is there shade, shelter, movement, food, water, other horses? Is it just another boring, bigger box? This is just part of the often overlooked, yet, accepted aspect of the life of a domesticated horse in a stabling environment.

As you can see, the best place to have a horse is at home with you and the conditions of keeping that horse in are very important. Many people just shrug off the conditions of standard stable life because that's the way things are, but they certainly do not shrug off the questions about why they have `difficult` horses. With most lifestyles of work and little time, we often seek band-aid solutions. They are abundant.... and never ending.

The example of how to approach a child is how I can try to explain part of what NHE is. It can take time, but once the trust and communication can be understood between horse and human, then possibilities are endless. What may be new is how Alexander Nevzorov has brought this love for the horse to help the horse consciously make the decision to do what horses instinctively do in nature. To the regular horse world, the only thing that seems amazing is collection. However, we also develop the mind and allow the true spirit of the horse to develop.

It is also important to note that NHE is not traditional Haute Ecole. It is not a discipline being revisited. It is not just doing the same stuff without a bitted bridle. Many people can achieve similar results, but it is far from being NHE. The truth lies not within the final performing results, but within our hearts and the horse`s understanding and perception of how we ask and being able to accept the response. We are not aiming for any textbook position or response, but what a horse can give according to its capacity. A subtle nuance, yet, a huge difference. It is also how those results are obtained and why we choose to obtain them in the first place! That is the difference with NHE and why it simply will not work for everyone. I would hope that anyone who understands this, will know the difference if they see someone claiming to be demonstrating NHE by using any kind of coercion.

As I mentioned earlier, there are prerequisites that must first be met that are important for the horse. What do you do with them, and what do you want them to do, what are you willing to do for them?

I fully understand how this may seem like such a dramatic shift and change. I have been there, and it certainly did not happen all at once.

***

Looking back on this article now, I see how I may take what I have learned from my experiences, and what our horses do, so much for granted. There is so much more that I wish I could expand upon but I had to keep it short and simple. As you can clearly see, there is not a specific exercise explained in how to achieve harmony. Those who expect a concise answer are still on the wrong track. I hope that what I write could help people to understand this. For expectations and results, when a person really understands how to reach out to a horse without ropes and the door is open for real two-way communication, then what a person wanted as results is no longer of any importance. As Alexander states, "The secret of your relationship with a horse is that you must love her essence... You must feel her pain, fright and discomfort as your own. You must love her viewpoint and try to share it. The secret of a horse's soul is that a horse owes you nothing and has no need to obey you". Reaching that point gives us a new understanding and respect for the horse from a new perspective. The idea of `training` is dissolved. Ironically, that is when all becomes possible.

In the article, I mention riding my horses, but after achieving collected riding and performing various Haute Ecole moves, I stopped regular riding sessions. Despite my desire to keep up schooling and exercise over the winter, it rarely worked out. The cold temperatures and conditions at my place were just too much. The winter days would go by with my increasing anticipation of spring. Finally, when warmer days arrived and the snow was all gone, I would have an urge to ride. Having the communication, willingness and power of the horse under me in natural collection was beyond comparison to any other usual riding I had done before. However, the winter was long and we were both out of shape. I would decide to get out there and get active again with the horses so that I could mount again with a clearer conscience. By the time the horses had the refresher course, both of us were getting stronger, back into activity through practice, games, and learning, the urge to ride would disappear. After spending much more time with them and seeing their characters and interaction flourish again, riding became just a tiny part of what was possible.

Just as old training notions haunted us at the beginning, we found ourselves still shaking them off as we went along. It may have been Haute Ecole, and important to point out again, it was *Nevzorov* Haute Ecole style, and despite the schooling without any force or restraints, did not the horses end up doing the same in the end anyway? The horses did have a choice in the matter, but why did we still pursue that goal of riding? With focus on the health of the horse in all aspects, how could we justify that riding is in anyway beneficial to the horse? Any honest veterinarian will tell you that horses should not be ridden. However, since they are anyway, then out come guidelines for the best saddle fit, new saddle designs, saddle pads, and the ensuing pharmaceutical products or massage techniques to help the horse with all its problems.

For typical riders who wanted to pursue NHE, the first step required was to stop riding for as long as a period of up to a year to allow the horse to heal. During this time, we built a relationship and new communication and allowed the horse to grow strong through play and exercises. Then what? Repeat what caused damage to the horse in the first place?

I began to consider this regarding one of our horses. From the time that we got him to two years later, his back significantly improved, at least visually, on the outside. Sunken muscles along the withers and back filled out and developed nicely. We had adopted him and although no particular back problem was pinpointed, there was always a cricking sound from the fifth cervical vertebra when he raised his neck up from grazing. I knew he was quite willing to allow me to ride, but I began to question myself if I would just because I could. For the first time, I began to consider whether it was fair for any of the other horses.

Alexander had been pondering the riding question from the horse's standpoint for some time. Riding time was already limited to under 12 minutes, then was reduced further a couple of times, and finally, Alexander stopped riding altogether. Thanks to the Nevzorov Research Center, his reasons went a little further than mine did by providing solid proof. It was science, once again, that picked apart the initial belief that the power of natural collection was enough.

At the beginning of NHE, his goal was to ride only a horse that was in natural collection. It is important to point out, due to several comments that I received, that the horse was not in collection as soon as our toe touched the stirrup. We would ask for collection, or the horse would do it by choice, just before going into any exercises. On the outside, it was apparent that the horse carried himself much better and was capable of doing more athletically. It is like the difference between someone standing on a street corner waiting for the light to change and a ballet dancer in position to catch another dancer.

Despite the incredible health and strength of his horses, discovering tissue damage on the inside of other horses, caused by riding, to the subcutaneous muscles cutaneus scapulobrachialis, and cutaneus maximus, he felt saddened to have promoted riding at all. Alexander holds true to his findings and when it comes to the welfare of the horse, there are no compromises.

I do not expect any of these findings or arguments to suddenly put an end to riding horses, but think about the following anyway. Saddles are supposedly distributing weight, but that weight is causing pressure on the back of the horse. It is not only the weight of the saddle. If you put a saddle supported on a scale, you can read the weight; however, that alone is not the true weight. Attach a cinch strap to the saddle, pass it under the scale, as if it were a horse, back to the saddle and tighten it. What does the scale go up to then? There is already substantial pressure not only to the surface skin, but also to the muscles underneath. Then add the rider. As an impromptu curiosity, I tried this with an old bathroom scale. The support for the saddle only raised the lower part of the saddle about two hands from the floor. I think there would have been a more accurate cinch pressure from tightening if I was standing upright but this gives a good ballpark figure. A thirty-six pound, or sixteen kilogram saddle became one hundred forty-two pounds or sixty-four kilograms. That does not include the pressure produced from the cinch strap.

We cannot lean on an elbow or cross our legs for extended periods without feeling discomfort or numbness. Another parallel to help understand what happens is the example of cause and effect of pressure sores, or commonly known as bed sores in humans.[4] The same is true for the back of a horse. The skin and muscle tissue quickly suffer ischemia or the lack of blood and oxygen. Cells start dying off. Tissue begins to necrotize. As we well know, the worst problems can arise from acute infection of the skin's connective tissue extending to bone and joints or blood infection. A very fit horse with better capillary pressure might hold off a little longer, but the same effect of ischemia is inevitable. Any slight muscle weakness is compensated for and the effects cascading through other muscles subsequently affect vertebrae, nerves (commonly subluxation) and eventually the overall well-being of the horse down to a cellular level. If we do not see blood or bones sticking out, we tend to believe there is nothing wrong.

Most riding horses do not end up with a visually evident serpentine spine or vertebrae that look like mountain ranges, but many do, and I have seen people still riding them and the horses continue to carry them. Nevertheless, it is this kind of medical information that reminded Alexander about the facts of the horse as opposed to his own passion of riding. Alexander's resulting decision strictly in favour of the welfare of the horse serves as a perfect example of why NHE is considered extreme. Old leather saddle or featherweight synthetic, even no saddle and adult rider or child, the result is ischemia just like us slightly leaning on our elbow.

To many people this argument may seem lame because the horses do not seem to be. We are so accustomed to seeing horses being ridden. We are raised with those images and can see it throughout history. What would the difference be if I put on a backpack and went hiking for two hours? First of all, it is my own choice. My body would react the same way, although strain and pressure would not be as intense. I am also capable of making a lot of little weight shifts of the backpack. Horses cannot do that with riders. Standing upright, we are capable of supporting weight better through our skeletal structure than if the same trek was done on hands and knees. Our spine would then be subject to gravity by perpendicular imposed weight. It might be rough, but recovery is possible. If it was done regularly, upright or not, and whether I enjoyed it or not, that type of strain would begin to take its physical toll on the body in different ways.

Ask a ballet dancer about choosing to endure pain and the inevitable ensuing development of acute and chronic ailments.

Human drawn rickshaws have been outlawed in many countries due to the welfare of the workers. Work or necessity aside, we can choose to push ourselves to athletic perfection, but horses are often pushed to the limit. Quebec has some of the best rules, laws and monitoring for horse drawn carriages, yet, in July 2010, a horse that completed five tours of the city had to be euthanized after collapsing from a heart attack on the way home due to exhaustion and dehydration. These type of stories happen everyday, and do not only appear in news headlines. At home, two riders came galloping across the adjoining field calling out for help because a horse collapsed on a trail after the rider pushed him on through wet spring snow and mud. Such examples are endless and happen all over the place, not just third world countries.

The physical aspect aside, increasing questions from the public on how Alexander achieved what he did demanded more of an answer than the general reply of learning to communicate with the horse. Even my response of, 'Just try asking the horse! ', or giving the example of how one would try to communicate to a child who did not understand your language, did not seem to get across to people. They wanted a systematic method of how to ask the horse. Alexander made a video demonstrating how he went about things, but it was still too vague for most people. I did my best by giving examples, but the more I did so, the more it looked like, and people continued to treat it like, a training method. Again, people would see the video or my examples and think that was the specific method. They would forget that it could vary according to the character of the horse they know so well, easy means of communication that have been learned or established between the person and horse, and adjusting to every moment by listening to the horse as well. Variations of how I worked with different horses follows. There are many details explaining the process and related examples, so if you need a break, do so before beginning the next section.

Unlocking Learning

At a time when I did not want to continue standard training for others, this gave me something new to do with the horses and I was really having fun again. My best strong point was always the relationship. One of the exercises involved a lungeing whip. The object of the exercise was to have the horse understand that it was not something to be feared. It was not used for driving or striking the horse. It was used for pointing or touching to a hind hoof, for example, while standing next to the horse's neck. Many people say that a whip should be just an extension of your arm, but was it never used as a threat? In any regular training I have seen it also serve as an extension of anger, even if not striking the horse. The existence of this game was mainly due to how whips are generally used against horses in Russia. They wanted to change that. One of the rules presented by Lydia is that anger or even shouting was prohibited. When the horse learned and believed that you would never inflict any kind of pain, you could whiz the whip by the horse's head and the horse would not flinch. For those who only used it as an extension of their arm, I say bravo to you. With any regular horses, how many would not be bothered at all if a human cracked a whip in their direction?

Part of it also turned into a type of game by having the horse pick up the whip. At the beginning, what was funny about this is that when a horse would pick up the whip, and was in a playful mood, he would swing it at my butt. They would chase me with it or turn and, with the whip clenched in their teeth, swing their head at another horse that just happened to be standing right near us. They would drive the other horse forward. I thought it was hilarious, but at the same time, somewhat disconcerting to see that when they were relaxed and playful, they copied us. They copied what we used to do with a whip. I heard other similar stories that many horses, around the world, had the same reaction when playing this game.

For the exercises, I spent most of my time trying to find a way to help the horse understand what I wanted. It was mostly mimicking. I had to learn to slow down, not repeat over and over in a short period of time. It gave the horse time to think, and then came the frequent breaks for play. It happened more than once and with more than one horse that after a session with a student horse, an observing horse would come over and do the move for me. Some say that this is impossible because a horse can learn only through association and direct training. I think we should give horses a little more credit. Although such a demonstration of their learning through observation surprised me, I was not shocked by it.

We know that horses obviously learn words such as whoa, walk, trot, canter, so why do most people stop there and not believe that more is possible? Horses are also quite capable of cognitive thinking and planning. There are common stories about horses being able to untie the most complicated knots, knowing that an electric fence is bad so figuring out a way to get by it, such as carefully crawling under it. I see so many places that have acres of grassland, but the horse is put out into an enclosure that is filled with sand. The horse is standing by the fence looking at all the green fields around him. The horses must think we are nuts. Horses learning by observation to unlatch barn doors or release themselves and other horses from their boxes are common. Nocturnal horse activity in one barn did surprise me. I had noticed that one door to a box was partially boarded up on one side and with a padlock on the handle while the horse was inside. This horse had already learned to open the door to his box by sticking his head out through the bars and playing with the sliding bolt. The bolt had been tied, but the horse would first untie it, and then be able open it again. Once that was prevented with a lock, then the horse discovered maybe through deduction or limited options, that in the same way he could slide out the bolt, he managed to slide out the hinge pins of the door. He would get out of his box and release other horses. That is why they boarded up the side of the door where the hinges were located.

For our horses, there is a 100x200 foot paddock. This is placed on part of one large field. I make a separation in this way to allow for grazing rotation. I see some paddocks or enclosures that are examples of efficient fencing. Usually there are three rows of boards between posts. I only have two boards. There is open space on the bottom and a fairly wide space in the middle of any given section. When the horses would graze down the grass in the open field, the lush, taller grass in the paddock started to become appealing. Stretching over through the middle between the two boards, they would usually pop a plank. When they wanted to get into the paddock, did they just push on the fence anywhere? No. They went directly to the already weakened area. That was more than enough for them to pass through. In the morning, I would see the damage and telltale signs that a few of the horses crossed over to graze on new land. I would tell them to stay out, tell them that they were not supposed to be there and although I could not blame them, I was getting tired of having to fix that fence too often. They knew it. They also knew to get out of the paddock before I came out in the morning. When I would be trying to hold a board in position to re-install it, a horse standing there, watching me might pick up the hammer and pass it to me. After a couple of seasons of this, I noticed that they would still reach through the fence, but not put pressure on it. If I called from afar to back off, they would. What is interesting now is that although I have yet to catch them in the act, I believe that they find a low ground and go under the fence. They come to the shorter section that runs alongside the house and again reach out from inside the paddock to graze the lawn grass, which pushes up stronger and faster than what is in the paddock. They know that they are not supposed to be in the paddock unless I open the gate, and they are as good as caught if they break or remove any boards, which they well know I do not enjoy. So now, it seems that my little commandos sneak in and then sneak out. I wake up to find them all in the field, fence intact, but their adventure is evident because an area of lawn is suddenly shaved right down along the fence line near the house. I see skid marks in the paddock grass, too. They must jump around in joy thinking, 'We did it! '. I am proud of them and if they do not give me extra work, I make no efforts to ensure that they cannot get in or out, depending which way you look at it. That is how well the horses learned about my likes and dislikes and a small example of how smart they can be.

These kinds of interactions and time allowed us to learn about each other. One of the basic foundations of movements for NHE was showing a horse where to place a hoof. I would say, 'step', touch the horse's fetlock, and place my own foot forward. After seeing how the horses played with a whip by chasing other horses, I discarded it. I liked Alexander's idea of using a brittle twig of Hawthorne instead. If, in the movement of the horse or my own, the twig would connect with the horse, the twig would break. I like the fact that it is part of nature and common in North America, too. Any fragile twig or long stem would suffice.

With one horse, wherever I touched him, he moved into my touch. Was he trying to claim my space and being dominant? No, of course not. In addition, I was not assuming that he had to move away from me in the smallest way by reversing roles. That type of horse behaviour remained between horses but no longer applied to our relationship.

It was obvious that he was trying to figure out what I was trying to show him. I went in with a fixed idea of how he was to learn my language, but I went with his reaction and we created a new dialect instead. Therefore, I would point forward, say 'step', touch the front of his leg, if I had to, and place my own foot forward. Touching him in the front was much clearer to him and he moved his leg forward. Now this was clear, and eventually, simply pointing in front of a particular hoof and saying 'step', he would move that corresponding hoof to where I pointed. Further, on, we could discontinue the pointing, no word, just moving my left leg would result in his moving of the left leg. Alternatively, just looking at a leg and extending out one of my fingers, he knew what I wanted. These little exercises not only help us to understand each other, but also are building blocks to a combination of such little moves and the beginning of slowly stretching the muscles to attain them with ease.

Once the horse could place his hoof, then I start to ask to place it on a raised object. The height increases slightly every week. When the horse could easily, lightly place the hoof on a barrel lying sideways, I would ask to hold that position. A two-tone whistle of high-low translated to hold, or freeze or do not do anything else. This should also be practiced in conjunction with walking and stopping. Once the horse stops, he remains at a standstill. For the raising of the leg, I would touch and hold the twig to the horse's knee while doing this. Eventually, I was able to slide the barrel away and the horse would maintain the leg up and forward to reach the twig. The twig is not used to push or cause pressure, rather, the horse knows it is a marker to reach and moves into it.

If this did not go well with another horse, I would hold the twig just in front of the knee while the horse was standing still. I would ask for the leg forward and then the knee would connect to the twig if the leg moved just slightly. I would be happy and praise the horse. From there, every subsequent time that I asked for the leg forward, the twig would be moved a little further away. Continuing to advance on those initial little moves and signs, when positioning the twig in front of the right leg at about chest height of the horse, the right leg came up to meet the twig. The horse understood so we did not repeat this a dozen times. I would ask the right, the left and then praise the horse and scratch the withers, give a big hug, then run, and play. The frequent breaks and play are very important. We could go across the field to where I hid some carrots and for the horse; it was like an ice cream cone to a kid.

One of the first things that Alexander would do with his horses is to teach them to sit. It was not for the effect of a trick. It is to help stretch the back and loin muscles in preparation for better collection. How he starts this particular move is clear in his videos, but he never directly mentioned it. Not many people seem to notice it. I also explained the tip to people, but as far as I know, no one ever tried it. I give the answer, but somehow it continues to get lost in the search for answers.

In a manege, I hope that the sun shines through somewhere, sometime. That warm spot in the sand is where the horse will roll. Do you remember the aforementioned two-tone whistle of high-low? After the horse rolls and is about to get up with the two forelegs extended, do the whistle. The horse freezes in between lying down and getting up. Maybe you could touch him and just say, 'stop'. The horse should have already learned how to react to a cordeo. A cordeo is a soft strap or rope that goes around the horse's neck. It should lie over the withers to just about the center of the horse's chest. Since NHE, decorative necklaces for horses have cropped up for sale all over the internet. I started with an old dog leash. I found the best was a single strand of a cotton lead line. Decorate it if you want. With the cordeo, you could help the horse slowly to rise up a little further. Again, the cordeo is to be used in combination with the two-tone whistle to stop again along the way. It may not happen the first time, but going along with what the horse does naturally is the best way to proceed.

A separate exercise was simply to ask for a walk from a standstill and then stop. It does not seem like much but it is very important. Actually, none of these exercises seems like much and that is why they are so easy. Then add what the horse learned about raising a leg and ask for walk. What does that start to look like? Spanish walk. In conjunction with this, again as a separate exercise, was also the flexing at the poll to put the horse on the vertical. (Being on the vertical means that the horse rotates his head forward, or tilts it from the neck so that the forehead and nose line are vertical to the ground. The movement is similar to a person lowering their chin toward their chest. It is a prelude to working toward real collection) When the horse would understand this and hold the position, I would ask the horse to bring in the hind legs further under the body. This quickly improved the horse's understanding and it would not be long before real collection would begin to appear. They soon did it on their own. It became easier and the horse became stronger. What they would normally do at liberty by spontaneous instinct, they now made a conscious decision to do in order to facilitate any move.

The horse would get used to a particular exercise, but was not always instantly fluid when another was put into conjunction with it. I recorded on video the first day that I tried to put two moves together with Peppy. It was for Spanish walk. He understood very well the jambette and to walk and stop. Jambette is when a horse is standing still and raises a leg forward and up so that the radius, or the part of the leg between the shoulder and the knee, is parallel to the ground. When I first asked for the jambette and then a walk, they remained distinct. He would first put his leg down from the outstretched position while stationary and then start walking. When I asked again for the jambette and then walk, he stretched a little forward because I stayed slightly ahead of him, but he began pawing at the ground in frustration. It did not easily register for him to put the two together, to raise that leg high in conjunction with the first step. I did not insist, or get angry or frustrated. I invited him to run. He did not run with me, he ran away. I waited about a minute and then called him back. He trotted up to me and was ready to try again. Finally, he did understand and took one great step and a second weak one. The barrier had been breached.

Leo was the first horse that I rode in full collection. Actually, he was the first in full natural collection. Peppy had done it with the Bitless Bridle, but I never did the common error of trying to flex at the poll only. He went into collection on his own on a loose rein. When people used to come for demonstrations of the Bitless Bridle, they would ask me how I got him to do that. Honestly, I do not know. If that is not an exception with most horses, then so be it and all the better for Peppy.

I noticed that there were two factors that come into play during willing cooperation and natural collection during exercices. The two are concentration and physiological responses within the horse. The appearance of pinned ears sounded only one reaction to outside observers; the horse was aggravated. Do not forget that the main phrase within NHE is

'The horse is always right'. If the horse was aggravated and did not want to participate, the horse was also aware that walking away at any time was an option. From my own experience, if I noticed that a horse was doing something considered unpleasant only to please me, I would have released the horse from the class. It has been rare for me to have a horse decide to leave after volunteering from a herd of five horses loose all together on our land. At the beginning, execution of exercises that demanded concentration and physical strength, the ears would be slightly pinned during the movement. In the moment before going into the move, or in subsequent steps, there might be a swishing of the tail. This was the horse making the decisions and subsequently, the exertions. This is my own interpretation based on my horses, and these are not just nice words to explain the reaction away. If I broke the class due to suspected annoyance, and I have, the horse came to me while I was walking away and still wanted to try again. I have also adjusted the way I ask. I have come to understand that reaction, in that situation, similar to a cat moving the tail while calculating a jump.

Eventually, when the horses easily went into natural collection, became increasingly fit to easily achieve any of the moves, including those with a rider, the ears were attentive and the entire face was very relaxed. The progressive changes that I saw through series of photos with Phantom, Pepper, Peppy and Leo were astounding. The pinned ears were still common in the exertion of airs above the ground.

The second reaction that I noticed was that as a result of the posture of natural collection, the horses often would have an erection. This was, at first, a physiological response to the position attained by the horse. Going into collection certainly got them pumped up, but they also developed and maintained a level of self-control. Through further concentration and the different context of collection by putting together a series of learned moves, this obvious physical reaction subsided.

I can tell you that when a horse would seem frustrated, demanding and aggressive with those pinned ears, in the typical observed and commonly known sense, was in the early days when we gave too many treats. It was not thinking, learning, understanding and curiosity by the horse of what may come next, it was the sole desire and demand for a quick palatable reward.

How can one completely eradicate the possibility that a horse may only want to engage in a class without ulterior motive? Let them be fully appeased so that if you were to walk across the field with a bucket of carrots, not one horse would be overly enticed by it. How many domesticated horses do you know that are not craving for the next meal? It is not a matter of stuffing the horses before a class. That would be counter-productive. It is literally their contentment and accustomed knowledge of the fact that they lack for nothing. If we look at human history, some of the greatest expansions for positive discovery and advancements, both scientific and artistic, were during periods of abundance. The lack of the need for survival mode enhances personal development beyond the realms of daily existence.

For the exercises, Leo was great in-hand, and I had taught him a signal for collection of three light taps on the side of his withers to go into it. I also used the word, 'axxa'. The word came from Alexander. It is just because it is a soft word, and my assumption is that it is possibly from Pythogoreas of A times A. In a sense, the bigger part comes from the sum of all parts. It is a good way to describe collection in a horse. The word is not important. It could be any sound or word.

I warmed him up on the ground and he did great. Then when I mounted and asked for walk and then collection through the three taps... nothing. Three taps and 'axxa' - nothing. I dismounted and took him in-hand again with the three-tap signal and the vocal cue of 'axxa'. He did it as usual. It took a couple of tries again for him to do the same thing with me in the saddle. Those slight changes, like me being in the saddle instead of the on the ground, left the horses wondering a little if they were supposed to do the same thing as before. After the successful ride with Leo, he would go into collection when he came up and stood beside me, whether I asked him or not. I wonder if he was saying, 'See? 'I can do it anytime!'

For half-airs or airs above the ground, I found that the simplest way was to try to direct the exuberance of the horse during play. Remember? Using what the horse does naturally. For example, running around with the horse and playing tag, or taking turns chasing each other. When the horse would be running to me or coming from behind me, I would turn suddenly and make an upward gesture using my whole body. It did not have to be exaggerated. In Alexander's films, you can see the subtle moves all the time, if you look closely. This movement would usually cause the horse to stop and rear slightly. When this happened, I would say, 'hup'. It did not take long for the horse to understand what I wanted when I would eventually use the cordeo signal in an upward movement and repeated the word, 'hup'. Keeping the twig high near a foreleg, would help to relate that I wanted the horse to stay up there. I wanted to keep that connection to the twig. Another possibility was when the horse was on hind legs, I could use the understood two-tone whistle, meaning, 'stay like that - don't do anything else'. This takes practice, but every second of improvement is an improvement.

A pirouette was easy to get, especially with Phantom. She was great at small levade, and it did not take long to add the cordeo signal to have her turn at the same time. The levade takes more strength and control. It is like doing half a sit up instead of thrusting forward into a full sit up. Practicing this from the ground is called cadran. It is a French word for clock or face of a clock. We would be in the middle of four cones placed around us that represented twelve, three, six and nine. Starting by facing twelve, we would try to get an up and rotating movement of only the front of the horse toward the cone representing three. The horse is to swing to the side while keeping the hind legs in the same position, as if the horse was the hour hand of the clock. Likewise, from a twelve o'clock position, we could swing over to nine and then six and then three and back to twelve. It was not perfect at the beginning. Even the word perfect is subjective because I would allow whatever the horse could give. With practice, a smooth, controlled upward lift, with collection happening all on its own, and a soft landing became a known routine for the horse. This all was possible from tiny little parts all put together. It just took time and practice and it was fun.

During play, I still wanted the horses to have a level of self-control and I learned how to act during my own forward movements to draw forth some of the horses' natural moves. This also took time. Eventually, the horses knew that I directed the game. They did not run uncontrollably, but watched for not only guidance but also my own spontaneity. I would sprint forward, and then hesitating almost to a stop and then sprint forward again, like a car bucking forward in wrong gear. What this produced, by accident, with Leo, was terre a terre. That is almost like hesitant, broken canter but hopping forward like a rabbit. Again, I could incorporate a signal that he came to learn what it meant and then reproduce it on request.

How I went about teaching any of those individual moves could vary depending on the horse. It could vary depending on the person trying to teach. Even in my attempts to explain how to do it, that only represented one possibility. There could be subtle nuances in the same described method, or a need to adapt to a completely different way.

It has happened on more than one occasion that I would be spending the weekend with a family explaining and teaching what I know and one of the kids would show up while we were in the manege. In different families, the ages of their children who popped in ranged between nine and twelve. After all my talk and examples to the adults, I would stop and ask the child to do something specific with the horse without explaining how to do it. No hints, no clues, nothing. I would just say, 'If you were to ask the horse to put his leg up on that barrel, how would you do it?' Or, 'If you wanted the horse to attain a semblance of being on the vertical, how would you do it?' It is still amazing to me that the children, who had not spent hours listening to me and viewing slideshows and videos or even seeing me attempt the communication with a live horse, would take only a moment of thought and then execute the move perfectly as I would have done it. In addition, they would often get a correct reaction from the horse. After a couple of separate incidents of this, when a child of the family would visit to see what was going on, I purposely did this as a private experiment. I would use the example to help the adults understand. Yet, for most adults, finding a way to communicate to the horse remained a complete mystery and great challenge.

The horse that others labelled as the insane, dangerous, worthless Arabian mare was one of the first horses that came up to me and demonstrated what she had observed through my lessons with other horses. She was always very energetic and as a result, quite athletic. As soon as I stepped away from one of the horses, she trotted into position perpendicular to me and gave a jambette. When Phantom showed me what she could do without me personally teaching her in hand, then we tried to cut right to the chase. I held the branch up to her chest level and asked her to step. I looked at her leg, raised up my arm forward as a mimicking gesture, and she raised her leg perfectly to reach the branch in front of her. Although she had just done that without any kind of help from me, touching the branch was important for me to show her. I asked that just once and I praised her and invited her to run with me back to the stable where I gave her a Cortland apple. That sweet, little, red apple is her favourite. Then we ran around together, chasing each other. Then I let her know that the playing and chasing was over for me. I still stayed with her and gave her my full attention. She rolled and grazed and while she went about her thing, I stayed with her and talked to her and lightly scratched her withers or sat in the grass nearby.

Important to also point out that she would, at first, slam her hoof down from a jambette. When I would give them good scratches, the horses would often want to reciprocate. But I am not a horse and do not accept, or cannot handle, their kind of mutual grooming. I would tell them so, and use the word, 'gentle' with a soft stroke on the side of the face. They learned this. After Phantom slapped down a hoof, I corrected her by indicating a no, asked for jambette again, released the position and asked her to be gentle. She placed it down softly.

I think that many times, horses are just waiting for that chance to prove themselves. Not in the sense that they have something to prove, they are different from people in that regard. They are waiting for that window for us to be open enough to receive what they want to show us or what they are thinking or what they are capable of, despite what we may have thought all along. They do wait for an opportunity, or often present it, sadly often unnoticed, to meet us halfway.

Phantom was bold and seized the opportunity when it presented itself. She would declare it was her time with me by warning the others to stay away. She could pin her ears and stomp and it was not aggression to me, but a reminder to others that she was not done yet and wanted them to stay away. I learned this by seeing the reactions of the other horses. Leo would even step in at times, from afar, and chase off a horse that may have intended to interrupt the time between Phantom and I. Sometimes, as in the past, her demonstration was directed at me. It was not aggression or a warning of her impending attack, but her frustration and a way of saying, 'Dammit! Listen to me!'

If I thought that I understood Phantom before and was listening to her, then with her entrance into Haute Ecole, she proved to me that I did not see enough. After that day, our relationship only improved. Did she change all that much? No, she did not. She made me really change. I had tried to analyze her for years and thought about why she acted the way she did. I did all this in my own little, intellectual world of detached thought. She brought out some of the best in me, or rather; she finally got me to get rid of that invisible curtain between us in person.

Leo turned out to be one of my best horses to work with to advance in Haute Ecole. At the beginning, I thought he would never get to any type of level, forget about advanced. He did not seem interested in almost anything that I presented to him, and I could not blame him. We had done a long road together, and unfortunately, I put him through at least some part of any new methods that came out in the horse world. I believed that he would be as a bump on a log, lethargic and uninterested. I did not ignore him and did try to teach him. It was I who was lethargic and uninterested. I thought the lessons would not progress well because of my own preconceptions. He saw that I was making an effort. It was an effort to which he obviously approved. He used humour to get through to me. He reminded me through some of his antics that it was supposed to be fun. We went gradually, but he gave me his full attention, really tried, and focused better, more consistently, than did any of the other horses. He was always waiting for me to show him what came next. He turned to games when he saw that it was becoming too much for me.

With Pepper, the Appaloosa, the way I tried to reach him was altogether different. He was adopted and a lot of thought went into accepting him because I knew that if I took him, it would have to be for life. He previously had an owner that went on trail rides with him but a problem arose. He would be good in every way but then somewhere between twenty to forty minutes of riding; he would buck like crazy and bolt off. At home, I left him alone and he knew I would leave him alone if he were unsure about anything. If I called him he would come to me, but as soon as I put a cordeo on him and wanted to show him something, he would want to try, but would become unsure, overwhelmed and bolt off. Again, a cordeo is a soft cord that goes around the horse's neck near the withers and down to about the center of the chest. It is used to make contact with the horse through light signals. It can replace a word or a hand gesture. For example, picking it up gently at walk would mean to stop. Simply, like a neck rein, it could mean turn left or right. From a standstill, it could mean shift weight from one side to the other. Two lifts or slight finger tugs could mean a levade. Three lifts could mean a pesade. It is a means of communication, not control. A cordeo will not stop a horse either from the saddle or from the ground. Pepper eventually made it clear that he did not want any type of equipment to touch him. The mere sight of a saddle would make him run off.

He had seen me working with the other horses and how we used a barrel for practice. One day I called him over and he willingly came as always. I just scratched him and wanted him to walk with me. He did but then slowed down and swerved behind me and stopped at a barrel. He poked his nose to it and looked at me. I did not hesitate. I dragged the barrel over to some shade and laid it on its side. I asked Pepper to come and stand beside me in front of the barrel. He did. I had nothing in my hands and he had absolutely nothing on him. I placed my own foot onto the barrel and asked him to do the same. He thought about it and raised his hoof, but only touched the side of the barrel. I asked him again and he just glanced at me. I asked him again and touched the back of his leg with a finger. This was too much pressure for him. He got nervous, turned around, and walked away. I was disappointed, but I let him leave. I replaced the barrel to where it was standing before, went to Pepper, just stroked his neck, and told him it was okay.

In the standard horse world, that would be seen as ending training on a bad note, or worse, praising the horse for walking away. I was trying to interact with Pepper and to show him that the way we did things was not what he was used to from the past. I was fully aware of that difference, but he was doubtful about my intentions. It would take time for him to see the difference. By letting him walk away and not forcing him to comply or punishing him was the first proof for him that I heard his voice. I knew he had physical and emotional issues and I was dealing with that instead. It was clear that he was interested in trying something with me, but it was also very clear to me how uncertain and fearful he was. Giving him reassurance and understanding gave him more confidence; trust in me, and willingness to try again.

The next day, when I walked into the field, he came trotting up to me. I welcomed him and praised him by scratching his withers. He perfectly positioned himself beside me. He looked at me with a shift of the eye and then repositioned his stand. He was thinking. He was telling me that he wanted to try what we started the day before. His demeanour made me believe that he understood what I tried to ask, and by giving him his freedom, he came back with willingness and curiosity.

Once again, I slid the barrel into place just in front of us. I decided to take it much slower, and to avoid touching him, I placed my right hand on the barrel, looked at his leg, and in silence, tossed my head toward the barrel as an indication of, 'C'mon move that forward'. He raised his right leg and placed it on the barrel. I let my happiness flow without being physically, ecstatically demonstrative. I scratched his withers, and hugged him. With all the horses, I found a way to scratch with a certain pressure and to find that magic spot that they just loved. I got the look from him that I often got from the other horses: a look of surprise as if he were saying, 'That's all you wanted?'.

I was going to stop there and dragged the barrel a few feet back to where it was previously standing. He walked over to it, on his own, and raised his hoof again and struck the side of the barrel. He had not exercised or stretched enough to get it right to the top. I pulled the barrel back down and into position on its side. Again, I put my right hand on the barrel, and he placed his right hoof. I praised him again and then proceeded to put my left hand on the barrel and he placed his left hoof. For exactly the same exercise I adjusted to what I thought would be comfortable for him and although it was different from what I had tried with other horses, it still worked.

There must be countless ways of how to inspire a horse or arouse curiosity and to get one single message across. Another example of how to achieve the previous exercise would be to use mirroring. Instead of standing beside the horse and wanting a corresponding leg from the horse to match our own movement, some horses understand better if we are face to face. The barrel is between us and a left leg from the person would have the horse bring forward the right leg. It is like seeing the horse as a reflection of you in a mirror.

This was a great breakthrough with Pepper. Did that automatically rid him of all fear or anxiety? No, it did not. Just like with people who try to positively deal with personal issues, he was dealing with it and pushing the envelope a little each time. After the exercise with the barrel, he was able to accept the cordeo, but I could not hold it. At least he understood that when I put the cordeo on him, we were going to try something together. While he wore the cordeo, I asked him to walk with me. He walked beside me but I did not touch him. After a week of daily short walks around the field, I slowly raised my hand and lightly touched the cordeo as we walked. I did not even grasp it. He was comfortable with that. When I could finally hold the cordeo, and he felt the slightest contact, he would not advance. I thought that was great if I was asking for a stop. I would raise it slightly off his withers and ask him to walk, but after only a few steps, the uncertainty would overcome him again and he would bolt away. I followed the same process as the first day working with him. He was uncertain about the cordeo; maybe felt that it was a restraint, so I removed it. We continued walks and trots together, but I kept my fingertips on the side of his lower neck. When he was able to consistently contain himself or not be carried away by swaying off course or running away in excitement, I made no fuss or big deal about placing the cordeo back on him and repeating the same routine. It was as if he never had a problem with the cordeo at all. We could trot together at a fixed pace with full self-control as I held the cordeo placed around his neck.

If the cordeo continued to be a problem, I would drop it from the work with Pepper completely. I would not be fixated with the idea that he absolutely must be able to do what the other horses do. I would work with what works for the horse. I would simply have to devise different signals without the cordeo.

There was always something new that the horses knew I was trying to relate, and without constant repetition, lots of play and reward at the end, they were always eager to see what was up the next day.

As previously mentioned, we learned early on that giving treats too often was a bad habit and came too close to operant conditioning, or what is commonly known as clicker training, or giving a reward for a specific behaviour. The actual clicker, a hand held box that makes a click sound when a button is pressed, is called a bridge. The bridge serves to indicate when the desired response occurs. It is part of classical conditioning, but I do not want to go any further than that here. Clicker training is a powerful tool, and despite protestations and arguments from the public in defence of it or to use it, it is simply not NHE. The result in the horse is different as it is in the formed relationship. You can see the lingering results of frequent treat behaviour in Alexander's early films when he winces when he gets nipped from a couple of horses who protest, 'Hey! Where's my treat?' To maintain calm, focus and real learning, a treat only at the end made the *overall* experience truly educational and pleasant. I love food and it can be a great motivation for horses. However, it is not so much the response that we want from the horse but it is to promote thinking. The goal is that through the observed, learned communication there is thinking and understanding. The response is a result of that.

Think of it as raking a lawn covered in leaves. You let the children know what task is at hand for the day, give them a great breakfast and then go out to do the chore. You are happy, enthusiastic and ask for their cooperation, and you make it fun. There can be lots of play involved at the same time by joking around, throwing leaves around at each other, jumping into piles of leaves and lots of laughter. It is a group effort. A family effort. The intended task is done, it is pleasurable, and icing on the cake, but not the sole incentive, is going out for ice cream afterward. That is a big difference from making your kids do something and in turn, they will only do it if they get an ice cream cone after every stroke of the rake.

I did not have the luxury of an indoor arena for privacy or to prevent distractions, but as long as outdoor conditions were right, they always gave me their best, unconditionally.

Although all the horses were loose together, I worked with one horse at a time. The motto of Alexander's school is, 'The horse is always right'. They are allowed to say no. I am also allowed to say no. When another horse came around and wanted attention, I would just say no, tell them to move off, and walk away with the present horse. Leo became my bodyguard, and after he would stop a horse from interrupting, that horse would duplicate the action by stopping another horse. Just like Phantom, they all wanted the individual attention. Eventually, while with one horse, the other horses would patiently stand together at a distance each waiting their turn and coming to me only when called.

Alexander caused a great confusion about this because he called it 'isolating' a horse. He also referred to a horse being left in a herd as becoming 'stupid'. Great uproar arose about those statements in the barefoot movement and those who knew the benefits of a more natural, outdoor lifestyle for horses. People forgot what NHE is really all about. NHE is the greatest advocacy for horses that I have ever seen. In *The Horse Crucified and Risen*, it is clearly mentioned about taking the horse out of the wild. He meant a real, wild herd. Not horses that we throw together in our backyard. The 'stupid' aspect was that, in the wild, horses would revert back to basic instincts. Seeking food, water, reproduction. Why would they need further knowledge from us or learn language, signals, identify colours, names of objects, communicate to us, etc?

NHE From the Inside Out

Working in this simple way was not enough to help people understand. I think that one of the main problems was for people to lose the 'boss' mentality. That is really instilled in us as humans, and in seeking a relationship, it is most detrimental especially when it comes to horses.

It was inevitable that Alexander's initial explanations of love and respect for the horse had to be replaced, in part, with scientific proof. Awareness and education about the physical side of the horse became a focal point. With Lydia's ongoing education in hippology, a new key phrase from Alexander was, 'The horse is an exact science'. For those who had a romantic notion or wanted to fulfill a long-held fantasy of having a beautiful, understanding relationship with a horse, this shift to science was extremely shocking or disappointing. However, nothing changed regarding how the horses were treated and the importance of building the relationship. A turn to science to produce solid proof of how horses and humans are similar in physiological responses may help people to stop many of the existing methods of horse training and use. With this proof being brought to the fore, it could clearly show that how horses are often used can be classified as abuse. Since many of the common ailments or the reasons for them and premature death in horses are so often overlooked to maintain an industry, the Nevzorov Research Center was created. The mission is to reveal what has been ignored or has not been fully studied in depth about the direct physical damage caused to horses by common, standard views, training, competition and everyday traditional use.

Lydia stands for animal rights and is vegetarian. She suggested that people would have better reactions from horses if they were not meat-eaters. Not only does a vegetarian diet give us more energy and clarity of thought, it changes our odour. This, of course, could have an impact on our interactions with horses.

It makes sense to me that my dog would find me very interesting if my breath was freshly emanating barbecued steak. It is not difficult to believe that it may be a little repulsive to my herbivore friends, the horses. It is not only the obvious breath factor, but we ingest the food; it is broken down and becomes part of our system. What emanates from our pores does have an effect on those around us. Humans, in essence, are not true meat eaters as carnivores are. Our bodies are not ideally adapted for it. We can eat meat, or choose to eat meat, and we have certainly been conditioned to eat meat as a norm without even realizing it.

On a physical level, daily red meat consumption is not healthy for us. It has been linked to rheumatoid arthritis, increases levels of cholesterol due to saturated fats, causes high blood pressure, blocks arteries and contributes to cancer and heart disease. It also clouds our thoughts and increases aggression. When an animal is about to be killed, the emotions cause a release of enzymes of fear and aggression due to imminent death and are absorbed by the flesh of the animal. If we are what we eat, then we are assimilating those horrid little molecules. It becomes part of us.

From an energy perspective, meat, fruits, vegetables, flowers, all living things have a vibration level. Fruits and vegetables have the highest vibration levels whereas in meats, the lowest vibration level is with pork. This aspect would be important for someone who seeks to improve his or her spiritual level and/or awareness. Foods that we choose to eat do affect us directly or indirectly. Effects can be instantaneous or caused through accumulation in the body over time. The most common type of daily diet or popular foods in present society is convenient but leaves much to be desired in terms of healthy nutrition. Being conscious about making healthy choices and avoiding processed food is a step in the right direction. However, it could leave one standing in a supermarket alley, looking around at all the stocked shelves, and leaving empty handed.

Kirlian photography[1] is what shows a type of energy field around objects. Those who know about the human aura, or a light energy around us, or what some may call our spirit, also applies to animals. A fascinating result seen through Kirlian photography was with a photo of a leaf. A picture was taken, showing the glowing energy around it. Then, a piece of the leaf was ripped away and a second photograph was taken. Not only did the section of leaf that was torn away show the energy, but also the leaf itself still energetically showed the part of the leaf that was torn away. It was like a ghost print of the entire leaf, even though there was a physical piece missing. Remember, that this is still a scientific process of any object conducting electricity and what is observed can be construed in different ways. Even though we can analyze it in detail, we do not always know exactly what it may represent.

In terms between science and auras, opinions clash. However, this view of energy flow is useful for healing arts, such as acupuncture. I find it strange that not much new has come forward since that photo in 1939. The only current research I know of is by Dr. Konstantin Korotkov[2] of the Russian University, St. Petersburg State Technical University of Informational Technologies, Mechanics and Optics. He uses a different method called electro photonics. When you eat a piece of meat, you are ingesting and absorbing not only a piece of flesh, but part of that aura or energy, which *is* the animal. Food for thought.

What Lydia and I refer to about scent goes much deeper than the obvious scents from the body. Before I knew anything about basic reactions from the neuroscience of olfactory senses, I was conscious of common courtesy. I spend most of my time with horses but would still notice a slight adverse reaction if, for example, I downed a cup of strong coffee and then went face to face with a horse. In an attempt to quit smoking, I discovered Tic-Tac. I carried those little mints everywhere. At one point, I was popping them so much that I was like a walking potpourri of mint. At least horses found me pleasantly interesting in their presence as opposed to unpleasant. That is something to consider, but avoid colognes, perfumes or heavily scented soaps. As previously mentioned, when I play with the horses, I am not concerned about getting a stain on my shirt. I will not stop to go change my boots or my pants because I have to go into some muddy section. I do not change four times a day if I have to do something else or go somewhere. I end up just like the horses, except that I do not wear it as well. It made me feel better to blend in so well and that worked for me, too.

As a side note regarding food, I must mention that I am not a strict vegetarian. If I have to eat meat, I prefer chicken breast, if possible. The reason is that out of the choices of meat and poultry, it is alkaline. What I mean by that refers to the pH in our body. Acidic is not good, alkaline is good. It should not be one extreme or the other, but slightly leaning toward alkaline. Where 7.0 is neutral, 7.35 to 7.45 is good. Foods that are one or the other are not always obvious through taste. It is how certain foods are metabolized by the body. For instance, lemons are at the top of the alkaline list. In their pre-digested state they are acidic, but not when absorbed and converted by the body. After a long, hot, dusty day, another of my favourites is draft beer. Out of all wines, spirits or other beer it leans more toward alkaline. Why do I consider that important? Out of all the studies and research there is not one in particular that I would point out because, personally, all I need to retain is one fact. In a laboratory, put active cancer cells into an alkaline environment and they are killed instantly. Cancer does not come out of nowhere. Often, one way or another, we create it. The list of foods and beverages that vary along the acid/alkaline chart[3] is extensive. I recommend that you look into it. Be healthy.

Regarding intellectual capability of horses, detrimental

effects of riding, or health of the human body or unseen energy, there are proponents for and against any information in all of those topics. If a thought occurs to me, that otherwise has no great bearing on my daily activity, the fact that it occurred to me in the first place is reason enough for me to investigate further. Most times, I find that I am already standing in the 'forest'.

To NHE or not to NHE that is the Question

I have mentioned the disparity about the dream that many have of owning a horse and then the common reality of daily horse life. For those who are lucky enough to be able to have horses at home with them, they are happy to return to a simpler life that includes the beauty of what having a horse initially meant to them. It is as if a completely new world opens up between them and the horses.

I had a couple of requests from Chile for me to teach NHE. In both cases, it was from individuals that operated a resort for tourists. One in particular had a package that promoted midnight trail rides on horses. She really cared about her horses and she wanted me to go there to teach her NHE. Now, remember that NHE removes all controlling equipment from the horse. We reach into the horse's head for real learning and willing cooperation rather than any topical, physical control. In this communication, we allow the horse to be expressive, encourage thinking and not suppress their character, but encourage development of it. The horse, to be willing with us, is also allowed to refuse. The woman liked all those aspects, but she made a living from her business and handed over her horses to strangers every night to ride in the mountains. This is an example of where I had to repeat what Alexander would tell people who wanted classes from him at the beginning and that was, 'Go to Parelli'. Actually, in this case, it was advice for her to remain with Parelli's method. It is not because Parelli is a prerequisite to NHE, but because she needed horses that would shut up and listen on those midnight trail rides in the mountains with strangers on their backs.

This example helps to explain that NHE is not just another training method. It really matters what it is that one wants to do with horses and why it is not for everyone. In that woman's journey with horses, she had reached a direct conflict with what her heart desired and the reality built around her. With that early statement from Alexander recounted in a story, it caused confusion at the beginning, especially since Parelli was highlighted as one of the world's prominent horse trainers in Alexander's first film. Like most people in the horse world, we also had experience with that method. Even I initially tried to justify it by promoting confidence through groundwork for inexperienced people with the seven games. As previously mentioned, we quickly realized this was very wrong in a NHE context, or treatment of the horse, and it was completely dropped.

Almost every trainer out there, from what NHE presented on the surface, wanted to add NHE as another feather in his or her cap. Seeing Alexander on a bridleless horse doing a pesade (horse rearing at or over forty-five degrees) on a magazine cover formed simple associations in people's minds. Usually it was the dramatic show that it seemed to represent and how it would be great for business.

Either it took time, or people completely failed to see, the depth to NHE. It was not the end result that counted; it was all that came before.

The first requests I received that were authentic came from typical riders who came from various standard disciplines with horses. The difference was that they had accidents. Either the horse could not be ridden, or the rider was seriously injured, or both. During the convalescence, by caring for or just being with the horse, the riders would start to see the horse in a different light. From what was described to me, they started to think about what they always spent time doing before the accident. Those thoughts began to create sadness. The accident and the down time allowed them to see a side of the horse that was either previously never revealed or overlooked. This came about from the simple task of treating the wounded horse daily. It could also be how the horse would act with an injured person just hanging out for hours. With riding being not possible, they began to wonder what else they could do together. They had reached this point through long reflection and an honest desire to make amends or certainly because they began to see the horse as a truly individual being.

The path with NHE and Lydia and Alexander, the people that I met through the forum, the evolution of topics and the ongoing research have provided a wealth of experience and knowledge. As with many others, it also demanded much of my time and dedication, both on and off the forum.

In those brief years, people the world over contacted

me in hopes of discussing more about the great changes going on in the horse world. We had been dealing primarily with the relationship and a different viewpoint, yet there seemed to be such a desperate hunger within people searching for a better way, not only with horses, but also within life itself. It represented a need for change, a need to embrace a new understanding, a need for love and acceptance. Self-development became a major part of the NHE consolidated information available. Perhaps, the plain truthfulness in horses is what draws people who are seeking deeper answers. In turn, we learn that horses force us to be truly ourselves.

I write these words because that was the predominant force and motivation of the majority of people who contacted me. However, I am just a man who shared my experience about horses. I am no saviour. In some way or another the key was love. It was love that was yearned for but never realized; love that was lost and nothing in all the world could replace it. In the other extreme, some felt threatened about losing their traditional livelihood, as if NHE would suddenly transform the horse world. Such fear and animosity and, perhaps, guilt were mostly present only at the beginning of NHE being shared with the world. That reaction was also common when the barefoot movement began to appear in stables. If a change of view toward the horse can be perceived as a threat to the existing horse world, then it makes me believe that the change in consciousness that I have witnessed is not only real but also widespread.

I have also endured people sneaking around my land, hiding, taking pictures, like paparazzi. I often wondered why people felt that they had to sneak around instead of asking me permission to visit or ask questions. It would seem that the self-created walls also exist between people. On the other hand, I received phone calls during the day and the middle of the night, sometimes very aggressively demanding detailed answers about the method and non-respectful of privacy or courtesy. There was one attempt to steal one of our horses and people inviting themselves to my home unannounced, or, travelling thousands of miles and knocking on my door, expecting to live here and me to teach them a new way of life with horses.

My life changed to what it is now when I decided to spend time with a horse again as an adult. In all that I have learned since then, but mostly, all that I have shed along the way, I greatly empathized with those who so desperately contacted me. I have often written how we, as humans, are too separated from nature and need to return to a big part of our inner selves. I felt too strongly their sorrow or frustration from common tragedies, heartbreak, and rejection in modern life. I had become more sensitive to it. Those people touched me deeply in many ways and sometimes it was too much to bear.

The experience greatly affected my life, professional and personal, for good and for bad, and I needed to remove myself from the public stage. Some who knew me may have seen that coming long before I did.

NHE has evolved and overcome the common adversity that comes with new concepts and has become quite distinct in the world. With riding not being the main goal anymore, it positively attracts those who want to learn about the health of the horse and the possibilities that exist with the horse beyond preconceptions and for real relationships. Others stepped up to keep the machine going while I was away, to lend support to others and to continue teaching. Through persistence, Lydia's mission has taken form as what it was meant to be. As the anthropologist, Margaret Mead once said, "A small group of individuals can make great change in the world. Indeed, that is all that ever has".

Bridging the Unknown

One of the most difficult aspects that I had to deal with was the unexplainable positive reactions that horses presented to me. Most notably as described in the sections, *The first Hint* and *The Day It All Changed* where all was going well and then a sudden break would occur. The positive part being what the horses did after that. I described erupting emotions and projection of those as a millisecond burst of images, scenarios, all tied up in a knot of my own feelings of caring for the horse. I have to admit that it would not be easy for me to try to duplicate that voluntarily. They were moments that just happened on their own. What I realized only later was that, in that moment, when I was already calm and not only accepted what was happening but was in accord with it, and honestly felt the emotion, it seemed to reach the horse and the horse reacted to it. The thought and action that the horse previously had seemed to disappear, fear or stress completely melted away, and they would voluntarily return to me perfectly calm and wanting to listen. I only gave a couple of examples, but there were others that combined the same burst of feeling or emotion or calm, clear thought and although somewhat less dramatic than those mentioned here, with the same unexplained results.

The reason why it was difficult for me is that I could not come up with a satisfying answer as to what had taken place. I certainly knew that something did, but there were different possibilities that, although I could imagine as possible, still left me reluctant to believe any particular fancy that crossed my mind. I do not claim to know the full answer at all. I do believe that it can be a sum of different parts that fall into place at the right time. Then I found a plausible part of the answer into which I did not want to delve. That was science. For me, I thought it would take the magic away. However, the more I learned about it, the more it made sense to me. The best part is that even though it has been proven, measured, and controlled, it still holds the wonder just like the miracle of life itself.

It was always believed that the heart responded to the information sent to it by the brain. Going back to Hippocrates there were those who believed that the heart served a much greater function. Certainly, that stress and different kinds of emotion affect the rest of the body in various ways. Dr. J. Andrew Armour of the University of Montreal discovered in 1991 that the heart has somewhat of a brain of its own. A network of about forty thousand neurons has been discovered within the heart muscle. It has its own memory and can act independently from the central nervous system. These send signals to the brain and can alter the state of the brain in its wave activity. It does this in four ways: neurologically (transmission of nerve impulses), biochemical (hormones and neurotransmitters), biophysically (through pressure waves) and energetically (through electromagnetic field interactions).

What is also intriguing is the continued work at the

Institute of HeartMath[1] located in Boulder Creek, California, that the heart can pick up information from the external environment and send us signals that can commonly be described as intuition. A situation may appear to our eyes and brain as normal or good, yet, for some reason, there is a funny feeling inside of us that is telling us otherwise. There were so many times, with horses, that I made a decision or understood something regarding the horse, without being able to explain it. It is important to note that intuition is best described as a sudden, unexplainable awareness rather than a feeling. It is not an emotion that suddenly floods us. If you have a feeling of fear, for example, that is not intuition. Rising emotions in us are linked to our thoughts. If intuition signals danger, that signal, of itself, is just something that suddenly occurs to us. It is then that fear can quickly follow due to our thoughts presenting conjecture based on that danger signal. With intuition, questions come after the answer.

What is interesting is that the heart and the brain can tune into each other. Furthermore, the heart creates a magnetic field five thousand times greater than that of the brain that radiates out and, likewise, can affect the rhythm and signals of someone else. Alternatively, someone can learn to tune in to someone else where the perception and communication can become much clearer. In other words, the heart rate of one person can have an influence on the brainwaves of another by bringing them into sync with each other. This communication is influenced by emotion and is most prominent when a person has feelings of caring, love and appreciation. Electroencephalograph (EEG) and Electrocardiogram (ECG) will tend to match each other either within one person or between two people; if they are in close proximity but more so when they touch. This tuning of rhythm between heart and head also results in improved cognitive performance. This exchange of energy into other living tissue also produces a strong theory about the practice of healing.

That, briefly, is only part of what has been studied at the Institute of HeartMath. Let me reiterate that I do not claim that such a sync between the horse and I took place, but it certainly may have on occasion on some level, or in another similar, unknown way, and since my awareness of it, more frequently in the present. This ties in with what I have mentioned about how we need to deal with the stress in our daily lives before we go out to spend any productive or positive time with our horses. In daily activity, stress and negative stress reactions like anger and hostility can become habitual. This increases the level of cortisol in our system, which is the ultimate stress hormone. The high levels can cause lethargy, diminish the immune system, cause heart problems, diabetes and increase weight. I think anyone who comes to the point where they want to explore more after having a slight taste of the greater meaning and appreciation of the life around us already has a very difficult time living the standard life. It becomes more and more difficult to go off to work in the concrete jungle, to get a paycheck, stuck in a box for eight hours a day. That standard life would become more and more frustrating, non-fulfilling, and grow in strength as a catalyst to change the job, lifestyle, even living location. At least, it was for me.

This is not something that was created in a laboratory. It already existed within us long before any study was done about it. Different techniques or names within different cultures around the world may have been applied to it, but only those with personal experience could swear by it. The capacity to tap into our personal awareness or, on occasion, recognize that something unexplained just happened must have occurred to every person, even those who are very unaware of such possibilities, at least once in a lifetime. A simple example of similar existing practices would be a time we sat in on a presentation by Twaminik Rankin[2], from Canada, medicine man and spiritual leader of the Algonquin nation. He opened up the ceremony with burning of sage and then passed around a small bottle of pine oil that each participant breathed in deeply. He asked that we focus on his beating of a small drum, which he said should assist us to go into tune with the beating of our hearts. Ancient ceremonies, meditation, or even a relaxing bath has similar effects. Even though a particular mystery has been explained by science, I find that it does not take away the splendid awe of it. It can help us to recognize and be aware of the world around us. This study reveals the potential we all have and as individuals how we can reach out, even in a non-physical way, be linked together or unified, create focus, understanding, healing, well-being, by bringing the best out of ourselves.

Plants have also played an important role for healing or well-being in our human history. On the medicinal side, the oldest experience comes from the Chinese culture. However, this was physical-to-physical (plant to human). The aspect that was often held in doubt also induced physical reactions, but was not seen, was the effects in humans or animals through olfactory senses or smell. This is very real and on the negative side, was tested by the military to create ultimate stink bombs in order to produce extreme various discomforts to the enemy. Vanilla is a universal calming scent to humans because of the relation to mothers' milk. To me, cat urine is not just an unpleasant smell; it affects my behaviour by making me angry or aggressive. It throws a switch in my brain almost instantly. Fortunately, I have noticed this and learned to control it. We have also learned that pheromones certainly work in the same manner as previously mentioned about the old cowboy's phrase, 'The horse can smell your fear'.

There is yet another example that goes without a solid explanation, but has occurred on a number of occasions with our horses. I would be thinking of a certain move that I would like the horse to make and I would be visualizing what the horse would need to do and how I would have to come up with a way to clearly show the horse what I had in mind. This is happening in the evening, the day before I plan to go out to teach them. I am breaking down the basic steps of what I would do to let the horse know that I want a shift in weight, the composure required, how I would combine a shift in weight with another movement like a foreleg lift, any words I might use or hand signals that the horse already understands or must learn. I am looking at any available pictures of a similar move of how the horse does this at liberty. Is what I am thinking possible in one move or session, or will it have to broken down further into segments? I am focused on this and delighting in the process and feel confident that the horse will be able to understand me. This is all before I even step outside with the horses.

It has happened repeatedly, that when I go out the next morning, when the horses see me, they come to life from grazing lazily or basking in the sun. They start trotting around and independently demonstrate little moves that I had been focused on the night before. These were moves that most of the horses had already been taught to some degree. My thoughts come to life before my eyes with different horses trotting in beautiful collection, doing piaffe, levade, or lying down. This is all going on before stepping into the field with them. I could chalk it up to coincidence and the horses were just itching to do something. There was one horse, and I remember the first time it happened, that raised his head from grazing, looked at me with such alertness, surprise of some realization and light in his eye, and did a capriole from a standstill. It blew my mind. I had never even come close to showing the horse those moves, but that is what was in the back of my mind. It was also a thought on the back burner of my brain specifically about that horse because I thought he had the best conformation to be able to perform that with such grace and power.

I often recommended to people to visualize what they were going to do, in detail, with the horse. Visualization works for athletes, especially Olympians, and I believe it helps create a certitude when we are out with the horses. There is no fumbling around or second-guessing when trying to communicate something to the horse. They will know if we are lost in our own uncertainty or doubt and it would only serve to break a focused connection between us.

The horse that stunningly performed that Capriole was the Appaloosa, Pepper. The way he looked at me that first time he did it, makes me believe that he picked up what I was thinking. As if, a picture suddenly lit up inside his head. He knew that I was so impressed by what he did; he would do it again almost every time I went out to him. I had to ask him in advance to relax and do nothing. A strong, large horse raising himself up onto hind legs and then jumping up into the air off all fours and thrusting out the hind legs without warning is dangerous for me, other people around or other horses.

I cannot explain what took place in that specific example, and to be truthful, it is not something that I have recounted to others before or promoted. It happened, it still happens, and maybe a large part of this mystery is simply the fact that my visualization and preparedness makes me a better teacher when I am out with the horses. That is what I tell myself when I try to make sense of it all.

Here I am trying to express something, that I have personally experienced, but I seem to be having trouble accepting it, do I not? When I was giving riding classes at another stable, all my students used the Bitless Bridle. I had students ranging in ages from six to sixty. However, the majority were preteens or teens. The horses used for the classes were all ages and they were the ones that were on standby for trail rides. They were rented out to the public. I rented them from the stable for my classes. When I gave riding classes in the ring, I never thought about how schooled the horses were. In fact, they were trail horses. They would take a rider and follow in queue. However, we did wonders in the ring. Week after week boarders at the stable would observe what children were able to accomplish with the horses. It was the one place where most people did not have much to say about riding bitless. From afar, some may not have even noticed the difference and simply assumed they were bitted bridles.

There was a woman who had decided to sell her Arabian mare. She had asked me if I knew anyone who might be interested. She found the horse too difficult and it was a constant struggle to control the horse when they were on trail together. One sunny day, during one of my classes, she interrupted and wanted to talk to me. One of her friends was going on trail and the woman was already discouraged knowing how her horse behaved, but she wanted to go. Seeing an eight year old doing dressage patterns with a trail horse without a bit, was enough for her to take a chance. She figured she had nothing to lose by trying the Bitless Bridle. She was desperate. I told her to take one out of my locker, and explained to use it the same way as a normal bridle, except, not to pull so hard. I told her to keep a slightly loose rein and to just clench a fist for a signal through the rein, and if that did not work, then to increase incrementally. Even an emergency rein would work; at least it would not do as much damage to the horse. I felt somewhat uncomfortable having to explain that to someone who normally rode with a bit. I also knew she was nervous, so I still wanted to remind her.

I continued classes and a couple of hours later; she and her horse trotted up to the front of the ring and called out to me. I was just finishing a lesson and was heading back to the stable, but she was talking non-stop before I got to the gate. She said that she could not believe it. It was the best ride she ever had with her horse. She had absolutely no problems, no struggle, and no difficulties. The horse would make transitions up and down even to a stop. She indicated how the mare was just standing calm while she talked. The woman's facial expression increased as she came to the end of her story. She had a mix of total puzzlement on her face, disbelief, happiness, shock. As if she had different expressions at the same time.[3] She thanked me and told me that if riding bitless made that much of a difference for her and her horse, then she would make the switch. I told her that she could use the bridle whenever she wanted.

I knew that she went to the stable during the week, but I would usually only see her on the weekend because I was there mostly on those days. When I saw her again, she looked depressed and she told me that she had sold her horse. The buyer was coming that day. I thought that her problem was solved since her last ride. She told me that it certainly was, but she was so used to riding with a bit. She could not see herself riding out all the time without one. When she had tried to ride during the week with different people, they convinced her to use the bit. They told her that it was safer and the only way to control her crazy horse. The rides were a disaster. When she got an offer for the horse late in the week, she accepted.

Before she decided to ride with my bridle, I had never had a discussion with her about it. She tried it and experienced, first hand, the great change in her horse. For the first time in two years, she was happy with her horse because she had a great trail ride. She was convinced all on her own. Unfortunately, she was conditioned to using the bit. Despite her own awareness, she did not ride bitless again due to pressure from others. They repeated the same thing that she was always told about controlling a horse. They were repeating what they were always told.

The day when she rode with her horse bitless and told me it was the best ride ever, became smothered from social pressure and disbelief. It was also due to her lack of understanding how both bridle systems worked. Increased knowledge through studies and documentation about the problems that a bit could cause may have solidified her personal choice. However, she fell back into what she was used to. It took little pressure to convince her to ignore what she had newly discovered. Even though something new was right in front of her eyes and she lived the positive results, it was too different for her to accept it. Now she was waiting to load her horse into a trailer for the last time. I saw, once again, that look of simultaneous multi-emotion etch its way across her face.

That always left an impression upon me. I used to ask myself how people could not accept what they personally experienced. Most people will say, "I'll believe it when I see it.", but sometimes that is not good enough. Now I found myself in a similar situation.

I think that it is also important to point out that our horses certainly know me very well, as I know them. We have spent a lot of time together, established well-understood methods of physical communication through enormous amount of interaction. We have had just quiet time together grooming or walking, picnics out in the forest, laying down taking in a warm morning sun, playing games that make them think of a solution, and just playing by running about together. When I write '...a lot of time...' I mean years of recognizing the most subtle looks and signals in each other. Would my focus and visualization work in the same way with a neighbour's horse with which I have not spent any personal time? I doubt it. Although I have never tried it. I have no personal history with or direct interest in that horse. If I made a deliberate effort to try it as an experiment, I would still have a fixed frame of mind that it probably would not work. Going out to see what might happen with a horse, I am certain, with that mindset and lack of true enthusiasm and authenticity, that it would fail.

I am mentioning all these things because of the importance of how such effects can influence our relationship with our horses. It is an awareness about ourselves and the world with which so much other life is shared. It is not simply the awareness, but being able to control it within ourselves so that we never are too knocked off our center. It takes practice, but being conscious of it helps to put things in perspective throughout a standard hectic day. The importance is to focus on the similarities within the world and of all creatures, not the differences.

When I was much younger, I recall flying over the countryside and an idea struck me while gazing down at the miniature world below. It was not much different in appearance or actual physical structure from when I would be looking down while standing on firm ground. Slight ripples or mounds in the ground, tiny trenches of water and life moving about. Being removed from the earth and looking at it from a different perspective, it may have been the first time that I realized that we are not alone or unique. Life is the same in different layers and it is all bound together.

When I first read the book, <u>Kinship With All Life</u> by J. Allen Boone[4], I found it quite silly. However, there were some parts of it that seemed to make sense and to which I could relate in some small way. Going through the book and being drawn back to it again, I found it held much more than his story of taking care of a dog while the owners were away and what he learned about communicating with this dog. Of course, that was his intention, but with time and ongoing experience with horses, I related to it more and more. I went on to read the second book. Although it is not about horses, it is the one book that I recommend to horse owners who want to learn about creating a better relationship. There is no method in there. It is certainly not a training manual. That is what people have to realize if they are talking about building a relationship. One has to reach out and be open to the other. It can be with people, with horses, or any other animal. It takes time for a relationship to develop. It must be honest or heartfelt, and although we may have the notion that is what we want, there can be no agenda. It cannot be made to happen, it just happens.

Remember that our own feelings or desire to have a two-way relationship and understanding with any animal does not mean that it exists instantly. Certainly, the potential is there, but it varies with each individual to which it is directed. I have some friends and then I have some very good friends. One relationship may start slowly and build strongly and some other may click almost right away and continue to endure and expand to greater depth. However, singular feelings of trust, love or oneness are not enough. For example, I would not jump into the cage of a lion that I have never met before. Just because I know of the possibilities and potential that exists for interspecies communication and great relationships, I would not throw my arms around the neck of a horse that has just walked up to me for the first time. It may seem obvious, but this is important because I have seen people who become so overjoyed, or overwhelmed, that they forget about the second half of the equation. I have also known more people than I wish I did who were so hurt by life events and society, that perhaps the honesty and beauty of horses drew them intensely. Despite the willingness and an aspect of joy or solace that they found, they carried too much baggage, too much hurt and were not creating a bridge, but only jumping up and down in joy, by themselves, on one side of the chasm.

Am I happier this way? Maybe I should not be surprised that a type of spiritual grounding or awareness or whatever name you want to give it evolved later in life after a hiatus. I had the good fortune of spending a lot of time in the forest when I was under twelve years old. Weekends and summers spent up north at a cottage. The scent of the earth, the trees and plants stirred something in me. I never analyzed the feeling or sought reason, but I would feel a different comfort laying in the middle of a forest, in silence, propped between large tree roots extending into the earth. It is not so long ago, yet the skies were so much clearer. Whereas now stars are visibly scattered among large dark areas of the night sky, back then, there were only a few empty areas within speckled, shimmering heavenly lights of all sizes. I would often sit atop a rock that cleared a space in the forest and gaze at the moon. The moment seemed to flow through me. I felt like I belonged. Nevertheless, a different lifetime unfolds and the years go by and with attaining what some may consider success, I was never satisfied.

I do not consider myself any kind of specialist in herbs or healing or spirituality. I have come to be comfortable with how I feel and what has led me further down this path is knowing what I don't want. In this way, if just riding bitless once upon a time put me outside the norm, then after all the choices I have made, my place in society is ever more recluse. Perhaps, I live in a bubble that encapsulates the beauty that I have found. I try to avoid generalizing, but materialism is so common in everyday life. The individualistic attitudes, the mentality of success by owning objects, the non-seeing of the splendour of life, and the brushing aside inner questions or thoughts that may surface in the stillness before sleep. Not only concerning horses, but also in the average consequences I see people suffer around me daily, saddens me deeply. When I leave my little green corner and venture out, I feel like an alien in a strange world and very far from home. Yet, I am happier when I turn my focus to where I see that so much more is possible. It is not a utopic world that I long for somewhere, someday. Mystery is already unveiled in plain sight. It was the stillness of the forest and the horses that showed me the way.

I never revealed my own experience about such things, but if someone with whom I was having a conversation mentioned anything about psychic possibilities or intuition, I would respond by saying that I do believe it, but I do not believe anyone who claims that they can do it. Although, I did lean more to intuition. Not understanding how it worked but having my own experiences, which I considered far removed from the regular world, I remained cynical about anything coming from the outside. I had managed to remove many walls inside myself, but also built up a few around me about society.

If I have come to accept a horse unconditionally, without prejudice, then I must allow that for what I call the outside world, including people. I do prefer my castle, but must accept the way the world is, see it how it is, and hope to be part of some small change for the better.

This is not about any type of thunder and lightning, earth moving moments. For me, it was usually very subtle. So subtle that it could easily be ignored if I did not pay attention to it. Here is another simple example: It was spring and the melt had gone. I went out to add a little more hay in the field to hold the horses through the night. I saw a few of the horses, but did not pay particular attention that time. When I returned inside the house, it suddenly occurred to me that I did not see Big Leo. The horses I saw were near the barn, so I just figured he was behind it. Maybe he was inside drinking. I shrugged it off. Not more than ten minutes went by and I suddenly had the idea that he was stuck in the fence behind the barn. There are old posts with cord that runs between them. Some sections have the original large grid wire behind it. It served only as a visual barrier for it certainly would not prevent horses from passing through. Does anything prevent horses from passing through? A five-foot deep ditch about six feet wide surrounds our land. I call it the moat. To a neighbour's adjoining field there is no fence at all, just a line of trees. Fence or no fence, they could always jump it if they wanted to, but they stay on our land.

I did not see Leo when I went out to spread hay and I told myself that I was just imagining something for nothing.

Right away, the first thought came back to me but with a sense of urgency. Not just an idea, but also a kind of tingling inside my body, though it was not actually a physical tingling. The best way for me to describe it would be like a swelling up or a sensation of a magnetic pull at my diaphragm. Anyway, out I went to check the area behind the barn and the fence line. Sure enough, there was Leo with his front legs through the grid fence. The new grass was just a little greener on the other side. He was standing still, he knew he was stuck, but I asked him to stand still anyway, reassured him and told him I would get him out. He allowed me to physically remove his legs from the grid to free him. As I held the flexing section of fence away, I asked him to back and he took a couple of steps back and stopped. I told him it was okay and that he did the right thing to call me. I went into the garden section that we have and pulled handfuls of grass and gave it to him with a big, soft hug.

I explained earlier how I believed that I have unknowingly sent out a message to a horse, but this example with Leo was the first time that I felt a semblance of that coming *from* a horse. Actually, maybe only the first time feeling it that strong inside of me. After all, it was Leo who first impressed upon me something I had never thought of before. It was the day he was rearing in fear in the arena and cast that momentary glance to me as described in the section, *The First Glance*. This last situation, however, was quite different.

When we first settled into our new home and had the horses with us, without thinking, we still followed the routines that we were used to when the horses were boarded somewhere. The garage was converted into a stable with five boxes and although the main façade of the property was well fenced, we kept halters on the horses. Everyday I would lead them out from the barn, one by one, to the paddock. One day, I questioned myself what I thought I was doing. There was no need for that anymore. This was our place. We were free. I was then able to go into the stable, where the main door was always wide open, open up one box door after another, say, 'paddock', and they would file out on their own into the paddock. Then I realized that they did not need halters anymore. I still brought them in at night. Maybe I was overprotective, but I was not comfortable with leaving them loose and unattended.

On an August evening, two months after settling into our new place, the horses were put inside because we were going out for dinner. By that time, the horses had been left out overnight before, but there was a big storm coming. I did not want to take the chance of leaving them outside in high winds with possible broken branches or any objects possibly flying around on the wind. On the way back home later in the evening, we were in the middle of a huge thunderstorm. There was lightning briefly illuminating the impenetrable darkness and earth shaking thunder. As soon as we parked in the driveway, I went into the stable to check on the horses and discovered that one was missing. Maybe the horse played with the bolt latch or I forgot to secure it before leaving. Regardless, the door was open to the box and Peppy was gone. I immediately ran outside calling his name but could not see anything in the deluge. At that time, Peppy's coat was almost all black which did not help in being able to spot him in the darkness. I went around back to the area described where I found Leo, but saw nothing on our land or by scanning the entire adjoining field with a flashlight. I started to walk briskly back to the barn not knowing what to do next. It was a feeling of panic, helplessness and rising fear, that maybe he was stolen.

A week prior, we had lost our little dog, Rupert. He always stayed on our land, but after he saw me go across the street to straighten out our mailbox, he ventured into the street the next day to investigate and was struck and killed by a car. That really hurt me. I felt it was my fault, but mostly, I will never forget seeing his lifeless body on the asphalt. One minute he was with us and then he was gone. How I so wanted to be able to take back a few seconds in time. We finally had our little green space, and this innocent dog was killed by venturing into the 'outside' world. For me, it solidified a separation between worthwhile life and existing society. The driver never stopped, as is often the case along that road for racoons, cats, deer, squirrels, chickens even cows. We all know how difficult it could be to spot a cow in the middle of the road. Perhaps the driver simply could not compute that he was not seeing things. In the local town, I once heard someone recounting a story of how he had hit a deer but just kept driving. Something caught his eye through the driver's window and looking down, was looking into the face of the deer that was pinned under his vehicle being dragged alive. Laughter erupted as he recounted the story. It is that complete disassociation and lack of respect for other life or suffering that just makes my heart sink. I buried the dog under a tree in that same aforementioned area behind the barn.

While I was walking back to the barn, I heard barking. It was a very distinguishable and recognizable bark. It sounded like Rupert. All I know is that I heard it. I knew it could not be the dog, I did not think it was a sign, or a signal. It was a sound that I found sounded just like the dog and any sound at that point while searching for the horse made me run back to where I heard the barking. It just happened to come from near that tree where he was buried. I shined the flashlight into the adjoining field again, and there was Peppy, standing right at the edge of the moat, on the other side.

Why was I so reluctant to admit any of this or even embarrassed to share with anyone else? I suppose it came from some first impressions from other people who shared with me their thoughts about this like the earlier example of standing alone in joy on one side of the chasm. They were so happy with their own belief and rambling on about it; I felt they were totally disconnected to what may have even been obvious, physically, right before their eyes. It always made me wary that if I tried to focus on a feeling about the horses, then, maybe, I just might be creating a story or image in my head or silent dialogue. That can be called fantasizing or delusional. My only experience came from unexpected events that happened with the horses. I did not seek it and I did not try to follow any kind of existing techniques. It did not seem that strange to me. Many people may not dwell on it, or pursue it further, but they could say, '...I knew it! I just had a feeling in my gut!', or the same for a mother's intuition for their child or animals that know when the owners are coming home.[5] It just happens and is a part of life. If we only just learned to quiet down inside and honestly, listen.

A trip to Hawaii had led to return trips. Two in one year. I felt different while I was there. It may be a glimpse of what we consider paradise, but it was how my thoughts changed while visiting different islands. It is not easy to describe, but it was as if I stepped out of a suit of armour. I seemed to be more myself and much more positive and proactive. Everything seemed so much clearer to me and the jungle foliage was vividly, energetically vibrant. Compared to a leaf or blade of grass back home, I found they seemed to emanate light from within.

Some research into why I felt different while spending time there helped me to discover ley lines, vortexes, and orgones. It is believed that the earth has energy lines that criss-cross the globe and intersect forming a grid that covers the earth. The trajectory of these ley lines connect many of the well-known unexplained megaliths or structures that still exist from a forgotten time.

Vortexes are spiralling energy in a given location. Relative to the ley lines they are geometrically equidistant around the globe. Like ley lines, some promote healing, and some can have negative effects. Perhaps, the most popular known today for healing is in Sedona, Arizona. One of the vortexes known around the world, Hamakulia, is near Hawaii. However, this is one of the places where radio equipment stops working; compasses cannot give readings, where planes and ships have disappeared. It is believed to be an area of strong electromagnetism.

Orgone is the flow of the earth's magnetic field that flows through the earth, out into space, and completes a circuit through the earth's poles. This energy is also associated with water beneath the earth, such as movement due to volcanic activity. Volcanoes also become portals for this energy flow. These energetic influences are primarily studied in Feng Shui.

These are very general and basic explanations regarding those three energy flows of the earth. Although what is considered a bad vortex is near Hawaii, the islands are not in it. The ley lines that cross Hawaii are believed to have the positive energy. This is why many people have an experience somewhat similar to mine. It is grounding or reconnecting to ourselves with a sense of emotional or spiritual healing.

Why would I make mention of such topics within a book primarily about horses? Whether it is clear or not, identified or understood, much affects the world around us. Horses as well as we are susceptible to much in our environment. I have heard stories of particular areas where too many bad things happened all the time. It could be a combination of a sense of confusion or unclear thoughts, various illnesses and accidents and death. These involved people and horses.

Animals tend to like areas of positive energy. If there is a favourite spot where your dog lays down, that is probably a positive ley line. They will also stretch out in the direction of the line. If you are in an area to witness it, the location or orientation would also be the path for migrating birds. The exception is cats. They are capable of absorbing negative energy and their cozy sleeping spot will most likely be in such an area. In areas of negative energy, an obvious sign would be trees growing in twisted or odd shapes.

The last time I visited Hawaii, I figured it was a great idea to stay. However, I was caught up in life again back home and those thoughts and feelings disappeared. There is an ancient practice from Hawaii called Huna.[6] It is the belief in the one source of life force. Like Chi in Tai Chi or Ki in Aikido. It is similar to different ancient beliefs that existed all over the world. Over a short period, those different beliefs were wiped out. The remnants of Huna survived better than Wicca, for example. The old teachings were affected all over the world such as India, Australia, and the traditions of the Native American Indians. There is a simple exercise of focusing on a distant point above eye level. Intensely focusing to the point where everything else around seems to fade away or become blurred. Then slowly letting in the surroundings through peripheral vision. This helps to activate the right side of the brain, unconscious thoughts or intuition. Stress, which is related to the left-brain, is put aside and then we are open to clearer thoughts and answers from within. Trying this exercise, or even closing your eyes and imagining doing it could help one realize how much is going on in our heads. It is not easy to remain focused and turn down the chatter or avoid other thoughts. Does not that sound like today's meditation and focus on the 'third eye'?

Conclusion

The best or at least indifferent reactions that I have faced have been regarding my own view from interaction with horses. If I state that my horse understands better if I ask in a certain manner, there is no refuting that. The person with whom I am speaking can only acknowledge the fact. It has no personal impact on them whatsoever. It can go further by the person telling me about a peculiarity pertaining to his or her own horse. There is an exchange of information, maybe even questions and suggestions from both sides. There is no denying that we love to talk about our horses.

Many facts that are presented in this book also present the most difficult task in the wave of change. For example, Dr. Robert Cook has put forth data on the detrimental effects of the bit on horses since 1997. His book, in co-authorship with Dr. Strasser, of barefoot fame, <u>Metal in the Mouth - The Abusive Effects of Bitted Bridles</u>,[1] was a revelation for some, an annoyance to many. The Nevzorov Research Center has put forth data on the physiological devastation to horses through standard use. They are detailed and not pretty. However, such information that is plainly presented as measured facts is often met with defiance mixed with insult.

I saw how things were done with a horse when I was a kid. I watched westerns on television, went to the old west theme park Frontier Town, and whenever I saw horses they were always decked out the same way. When I bought my first horse, I was also sold all the standard tack and I had no questions whatsoever. It all seemed normal to me.

Dr. Cook, Nevzorov, or anyone else who may provide research, provide intellectual arguments. What makes people change is not science on a printed page; it is the personal emotional factor from every horse owner. If people are happy doing what they are doing, they do not like to be told not to do it. It is very rare that raw data will change someone's habitual beliefs. If it does, it is because it touches a part of that person's emotion regarding directly or indirectly his or her own horse. A part that, for the person, is pertinent in that point in time. It must be already lingering somewhere inside. If it does not affect the way a person chooses to use a horse the reaction remains, nonetheless, quite emotional but is negative and directed at the author of the research.

It was when my planned idea of riding was taken away that I made changes thanks to Big Leo. Adjusting to him by initially using only a halter to ride allowed me to continue to do what I wanted to do. The small break from tradition was allowing and not prohibitive. The time for acceptance and change was right for me. Going through that experience helped me to begin to notice how other horses reacted, do more learning on my own, and ultimately, prepare the threshold for another change down the road.

During the different phases through which I went with

horses, I never tried to convince anyone about any of my beliefs. From training horses at the very beginning, adjusting my manner or communication to each individual horse, is what attracted people who would observe from afar. In the first year as representative for the bitless cross under bridle, I had placed an advertisement in a journal published by the Quebec Paint Horse Association. The following issue had a large part dedicated to bits. Large pictures, large text. They were screaming from the pages. I realized that I ruffled many feathers. It was the last time that I advertised. I knew that when people were ready for information or change they would find me.

I have become so comfortable with my life at home with horses. There are times that I am reminded that what I see as the colour blue is not blue to everyone. I have become so accustomed to how the horses are that I take for granted their everyday expressions and actions. I only realise this when someone visiting will fall on his or her backside in awe after a horse does something that I consider perfectly normal within our little family.

I also realise that my own experience has brought me what I was particularly looking for in horses. It was not a goal to find something specific, however, the results ultimately led to a way of life with them where I find a satisfying happiness. That experience is what I hold dear to my heart. I am fully aware that what I reveal within this book may not be the same type of happiness that others seek.

What I did worked out for the horses and me. Changes that I had made were incremental over the years and I understood that others would also have to live their own experiences. A change to topical equipment was just the tip of the iceberg. I know that preaching or pointing the finger to others will produce an intellectual argument that gives rise to emotions. Those two aspects can be positive if they are separated and distinct. Those two ingredients combined within an argument will only serve to negate any possibility of insight or learning. I can only praise and encourage anyone who shows any interest in doing right by their horse in any way that they personally feel comfortable with at that time. I have faith that those people will advance and grow in thought and in heart.

Looking at the physical aspect regarding horses cannot be discarded; however, I believe that medical research is only a small part of the discovery required in our journey with horses.

I do not believe that horses will one day be so protected that they are as crystal figurines that are safely locked away inside a display cabinet. Nor do I think it should be so. Such an image brings to mind <u>Aes Triplex</u> by Robert Louis Stevenson[2], where is mentioned a scientist fixated on preserving his health. He lives in accordance to what he believes is self-preservation by living in a temperature-controlled room, wears tin shoes and subsists solely on tepid milk. That is existence but it is not living.

Taking a break from the NHE forum, closing my website, cessation of writing articles and all consultation to the public left me a little in a state of limbo. I was so used to spending so much time working at the computer. It was difficult to settle my thoughts, emotions and to find an inner calm. We know that rapid switching between emails, links, websites, and chat can help to sharpen multi-tasking. There is so much information at our fingertips, however, there is more also known about how internet usage changes thought patterns in our brain. A former bookworm may develop difficulty in settling down to become absorbed in reading a book. Quiet reflection is diminished. The real world is interrupted far too often and tends to become sporadic and fragmented just like the virtual life.

I missed the life that I had previously so greatly yearned. Little did I realise that, once again, life was slipping by while it was present all around me. It took at least six months for me to wind down and to once again appreciate the stillness in a field of horses at sunset. It was after the pace slowed or appreciation of the moment returned that I realized that it had been missing for so long.

My intention was to write a book that would touch the hearts of all who read it. It did not turn out exactly as I wished. This is not fantasy and so the world creeps in oftentimes with the coldness of reality. Nonetheless, it is this diversity that allows love to shine ever more brightly when it is found.

There has been an improvement regarding the lessening degree of physical violence in the regular horse world, but when I look around me, despite the catch phrases of partnership, bonding, relationship, what I still see is an attitude toward the horse of do it - or else. In many cases, the term 'natural' does not necessarily mean not coerced. When most people search for answers and truth, what they really want is to hear what suits them. How often is the answer really coming from the horse? As I learned with Leo, everyone else's opinion is not what mattered, including my own. Those who are ready for an honest answer will find the horse of their dreams.

Going out to experience life and to discover the grandeur of all creation is what allows us to live a full life and to learn and evolve. The human spirit and thirst for life and knowledge has succeeded in discovering almost everything earthly imaginable. There is little in grand adventures left. It is no longer a question of finding a route to China, inventing the bottle cap or elevator or reaching space. The quest for ease, manipulation and domination within the immediate world has almost been fully appeased. With much devastation. Despite all that, there is still such on-going debate about horses. They continue to play a large part in our lives and stimulate something within us.

Whereas we can choose to take the risks associated with life, push the boundaries of our external and internal worlds, if we have learned anything, we can only ask the horse to join us in our journey. What the horses showed me was that the dream was attainable by turning around everything that I believed. Maybe, all along, they have been asking us to join *them*.

References

At First Glance
1.   Dr. Cook's cross-under bitless bridle
       www.bitlessbridle.com

Communicating Like A Horse

1.   http://www.parellinaturalhorsetraining.com
2.   http://montyroberts.com

3.   www.jneurosci.org/cgi/content/abstract/25/47/11045
       Ian C. G. Weaver, Frances A. Champagne, Shelley E.
       Brown, Sergiy Dymov, Shakti Sharma, Michael J.
       Meaney, and Moshe   Szyf

4.   Early Life Environments: Ian C.G. Weaver is from
       the Developmental and Stem Cell Biology Program,
       Hospital for Sick Children, Toronto Medical
       Discovery East Tower, Medical and Related Sciences
       Centre

The First Hint
1.   Anatomy of Domestic Animals, 4th ed. Edited by
       J.D.Grossman, Philadelphia, W.B.Saunders Co., 1953.

The Magical Forest

1.   Xenophon, The Art of Horsemanship, Publisher: J. A. Allen (August 1, 1999) Language: English
      ISBN-10: 0851310419
      ISBN-13: 978-0851310411

Perception

1.   Blink by Malcolm Gladwell. Publisher: Little, Brown and Company; 1 edition (Jan 11 2005) ISBN-13: 978-0316172325

The Crossroads

1.   Roger Sperry, www.nobelprize.org
      + http://viewzone2.com/bicamx.html

The NHE Experience

1.   Nevzorov Haute Ecole, www.hauteecole.ru
2.   The Horse Crucified and Risen, www.horse-revolution.com
3.   Natural Horse Magazine, www.naturalhorse.com
4.   mayoclinic.com/health/bedsores/ds00570/dsection=causes

NHE From the Inside Out

1.   The Archives of American Art Journal of the Smithsonian Institute.
2.   ElectroPhotonics, Dr. Konstantin Korotkov, www.korotkov.org

3.   Acid/Alkalinefoodchart (one example)
      angelfire.com/az/sthurston/acid_alkaline_foods_list.html

Bridging the Unknown

1.   Institute of HeartMath, www.heartmath.org
2.   Dominique (t8aminik) Rankin,
      www.dominiquerankin.ca
3.   http://viewzone2.com/bicamx.html by Dan Eden
4.   Kinship with all Life, J. Allen Boone, Publisher:
      HarperOne (January 28, 1976) Language: English
      ISBN-10: 0060609125 ISBN-13: 978-0060609122
5.   Rupert Sheldrake: Dogs That Know When Their
      Owners Are Coming Home: And Other Unexplained
      Powers of Animals
      ISBN-13: 978-0609805336
6.   Huna, www.ancienthuna.com

Conclusion

1.   Metal in the Mouth - The Abusive Effects of Bitted
      Bridles
      Publisher: Sabine Kells; 1st edition (2003) Language:
      English ISBN-10: 0968598854
      ISBN-13: 978-0968598856

2.   Aes Triplex by Robert Louis Stevenson, Publisher:
      Mosher; Second Mosher Edition edition (January 1, 1
      903) ASIN: B0026CSU48

About the Author

Thanks to horses Michael Bevilacqua left behind a standard life in the city to follow his heart. It was a reconnection to horses, nature and his true self.

Quickly drifting further from standard training methods he discovered the beauty and simplicity of allowing honest relationships with horses. Through his business, Equi-Forme, based in Quebec, Canada, he adhered to his own way of training and instruction and positively changed the lives of many horses and people.

To promote the welfare of the horse, he helped to build the international side of Nevzorov Haute Ecole and became the Senior Representative. As a writer, his articles have touched the hearts and minds of horse owners around the world. His horse training business has been replaced with educating people. Regarded as a true master and a gifted teacher he is sought after to give seminars that help to bring out the best in our horses and ourselves.

www.ingramcontent.com/pod-product-compliance
Lightning Source LLC
Chambersburg PA
CBHW062146280526
45788CB00001B/328